MARCIA L. TATE

For information:

Corwin Press
A SAGE Company
2455 Teller Road
Thousand Oaks, California 91320
CorwinPress.com

SAGE, Ltd.
1 Oliver's Yard
55 City Road
London EC1Y 1SP
United Kingdom

SAGE India Pvt. Ltd.
B 1/I 1 Mohan Cooperative
Industrial Area
Mathura Road, New Delhi
India 110 044

SAGE Asia-Pacific Pvt. Ltd.
33 Pekin Street #02-01
Far East Square
Singapore 048763

Printed in the United States of America.

ISBN: 978-1-4129-5925-4

This book is printed on acid-free paper.

08 09 10 11 12 10 9 8 7 6 5 4 3 2 1

Executive Editor: Kathleen Hex
Managing Developmental Editor: Christine Hood
Editorial Assistant: Anne O'Dell
Developmental Writer: Kristi Lew
Developmental Editor: Karen P. Hall
Proofreader: Carrie Reiling
Art Director: Anthony D. Paular
Design Project Manager: Jeffrey Stith
Cover Designers: Monique Hahn and Lisa Miller
Illustrator: Scott Rolfs
Cover Illustrator: Corbin Hillam
Design Consultant: The Development Source

GRADES 6–8
SCIENCE

TABLE OF CONTENTS

Connections to Standards

This chart shows the national science standards covered in each chapter.

SCIENCE AS INQUIRY	Standards are covered on pages
Understand about scientific inquiry.	8, 11, 75

PHYSICAL SCIENCE	Standards are covered on pages
Understand properties and changes of properties in matter.	15, 18, 23, 25
Understand motions and forces.	21, 29, 35
Understand transfer of energy.	23, 29, 31, 35

LIFE SCIENCE	Standards are covered on pages
Understand structure and function in living systems.	38, 44, 47, 50, 54, 60, 63
Understand reproduction and heredity.	41, 50, 57
Understand populations and ecosystems.	71
Understand diversity and adaptations of organisms.	41, 44, 47, 71, 81

EARTH AND SPACE SCIENCE	Standards are covered on pages
Understand structure of the earth system.	66, 68, 71, 75, 78, 84, 86, 88, 90
Understand Earth's history.	68, 71, 78, 81, 86, 88, 90
Understand Earth in the solar system.	75, 84, 90

SCIENCE AND TECHNOLOGY	Standards are covered on pages
Identify abilities of technological design.	8, 29
Understand about science and technology.	8, 29, 84, 90

SCIENCE IN PERSONAL AND SOCIAL PERSPECTIVES	Standards are covered on pages
Understand the importance of personal health.	63
Understand populations, resources, and environments.	44, 47, 66
Identify natural hazards.	68
Understand science and technology in society.	31, 75, 84, 90

HISTORY AND NATURE OF SCIENCE	Standards are covered on pages
Understand science as a human endeavor.	11, 84, 90
Understand the history of science.	11, 81, 84

978-1-4129-5925-4

Introduction

Think back to your years as a student. Which classes do you remember most clearly? Many of us fondly remember those dynamic classes that engaged our attention. However, we can just as easily remember classes in which lectures seemed to last forever. The difference is that we can usually recall something we *learned* in the dynamic classroom. This is because our brains were engaged.

The latest in brain research reiterates what good teachers already know—student engagement is crucial to learning. Using technological methods, including PET scans and CAT scans, scientists have identified which learning strategies best engage the brain (Tate, 2003). The results reveal that using games to energize students is one of the best ways to activate learning. Can students can truly learn content while playing games? Walk by a classroom where students are playing a game, and you might see chaos at first glance. Look again—this is actually collaboration. Amidst the laughter and buzz of competition, students are willingly discussing material once considered bland. When students are allowed to "play," they interact using all of their senses, stimulating brain function that helps retain content.

How to Use This Book

Correlated with the national standards for science, this book provides games that will engage all students, even reluctant learners. The games review concepts across the major science strands, including physical science, life science, and earth and space science. They also follow a format that promotes learning and retention, including focus activity, modeling, guided practice, check for understanding, independent practice, and closing. Using these strategies ensures that students are active participants in their own learning, not passive bystanders.

You may use the games to review science concepts, reward students with a "game day," or as a springboard for students to create their own. Adjust the games to best meet the needs of your students and your curriculum. Games such as Energy Bingo, Element Memory Match, and Solar System Scramble may be modified to review vocabulary for any subject matter. Games such as Energy Hot Potato and Human Body Quiz Show are ideal for reviewing entire units of study.

Games can be fun, lively, and spirited. The little bit of extra effort it takes to implement games into your curriculum will reap loads in student involvement. Just like the fond memories you keep of that dynamic class years ago, your students will remember the fun they had in your class and, more important, what they learned.

Put It Into Practice

Lecture and repetitive worksheets have long been the traditional method of delivering knowledge and reinforcing learning. While some higher-achieving students may learn from this type of instruction, educators now know the importance of actively engaging students' brains if those young minds are to truly acquire and retain content, not only for tests but for a lifetime.

The 1990s were dubbed the Decade of the Brain because millions of dollars were spent on brain research, helping educators and researchers alike understand more about the learning process in a young mind. But learning theories that address the importance of actively engaging the brain have been proposed for decades, as evidenced by research such as Howard Gardner's theory of multiple intelligences (1983), Bernice McCarthy's 4MAT Model (1990), and VAKT (visual, auditory, kinesthetic, tactile) learning styles theories.

I have identified 20 strategies that, according to brain research and learning styles theories, appear to correlate with the way the brain learns best. I have observed hundreds of teachers—regular education, special education, and gifted. Regardless of the classification or grade level of the students, exemplary teachers consistently use these 20 strategies to deliver memorable classroom instruction and help their students understand and retain vast amounts of content.

These 20 brain-based instructional strategies include the following:

1. Brainstorming and Discussion
2. Drawing and Artwork
3. Field Trips
4. Games
5. Graphic Organizers, Semantic Maps, Word Webs
6. Humor
7. Manipulatives, Experiments, Models
8. Metaphors, Analogies, Similes
9. Mnemonic Devices
10. Movement
11. Music, Rhythm, Rhyme, and Rap
12. Project-based and Problem-based Instruction
13. Reciprocal Teaching and Cooperative Learning

978-1-4129-5925-4

14. Role Play, Drama, Pantomime, Charades
15. Storytelling
16. Technology
17. Visualization and Guided Imagery
18. Visual Presentations
19. Work Study and Apprenticeships
20. Writing and Journals

This book features Instructional Strategy 4: Games. While playing games, students use teamwork, interpersonal skills, and movement and experience the spirit of competition. They actively express emotions, interact with friends, and explore new challenges of learning with immediate feedback and success (Beyers, 1998). The inherent joy of play is the brain's link from a world of reality to the development of creativity. In addition, play speeds up the brain's maturation process with built-in elements of competition, novelty, acknowledgement, and time limitations (Jensen, 2001).

Games involve active learning. The games in this book help students learn on a variety of levels. Some games involve quiet concentration, some energized, kinesthetic movement. However, all of the games involve interpersonal skills of sharing, discussing, creating, and working effectively with a team or partner. Once students are familiar with how a game is constructed, they can use these same ideas to create their own versions of the game. Brain research shows that when students are involved in the design and construction of a learning game, the game's effectiveness is enhanced (Wolfe, 2001).

Students are no strangers to competition. They face it regularly when playing team sports or auditioning for the school play. That same sense of competition and teamwork can take place in the classroom. Board games, card games, memory games, trivia games, and games that encourage physicality, using the senses, and creative imagination all provide the social stimulation, discussion, movement, and creativity that make students actively participate in learning.

These memorable strategies help students make sense of learning by focusing on the ways the brain learns best. Fully supported by the latest brain research, the games presented in this resource provide the tools you need to boost motivation, energy, and most important, the academic achievement of your students.

CHAPTER 1

Physical Science

Laboratory Scavenger Hunt

Materials

- Laboratory Scavenger Hunt reproducible
- laboratory and safety equipment (balance scale, fire blanket or safety shower, microscope or magnifying glass, lab apron or lab coat, lab goggles, fire extinguisher, thermometer, mortar and pestle, beaker or flask or graduated cylinder, Bunsen burner or hot plate)
- variety of mini stickers

Objectives

Students will identify and describe laboratory and safety equipment. Students will understand the use of laboratory and safety equipment.

Students conducting laboratory experiments and activities around the laboratory need to know the location, function, and proper care of each piece of equipment. In this game, students learn the location and function of important laboratory and safety equipment that they will use throughout the year.

1. Make different versions of the **Laboratory Scavenger Hunt reproducible (page 10)**, rearranging the order of the clues for students to follow. Adhere a set of stickers to each piece of laboratory equipment, one sticker per team of students. Use a different type of sticker for each object. Place an extra sticker on the balance scale for guided instruction. Make an answer key of the stickers used.
2. Introduce the game by asking: *Who has been on a scavenger hunt?* Explain to students that they will be competing in a special kind of laboratory scavenger hunt.

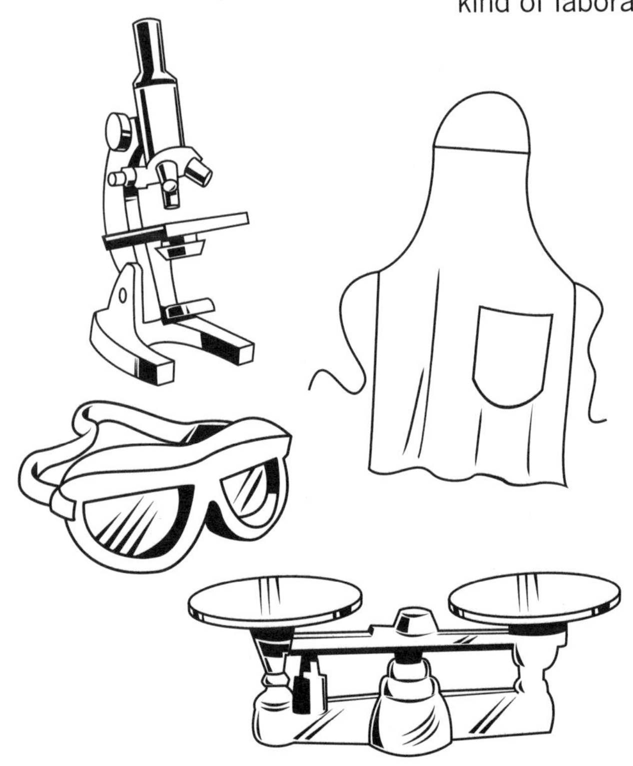

3. Give each team of two to four students one version of the Laboratory Scavenger Hunt reproducible, pointing out that there are different versions of the list. Explain that the object of the game is to find all the items on the list before time runs out and put a sticker from each item next to its correct clue on the list.
4. Demonstrate by using the extra sticker on the balance scale. Ask: *Which piece of equipment is used to measure mass?* Go to the correct answer, the balance scale, and demonstrate how to remove one of the stickers and place it in the box next to the correct clue on the reproducible. Make sure students understand that they should remove only one sticker, leaving the rest for other teams to use.

5. Give teams ten minutes to complete the scavenger hunt. If they finish early, record their time on their paper. The team with the most correct answers in the shortest amount of time wins.
6. After the game, review the correct answers. Invite volunteers to point out where each piece of equipment is located and explain how that equipment is used.

Extended Learning

- Have students work individually or in cooperative groups to draw and label a map indicating the location of all laboratory equipment in the classroom. You might also have them include windows, doors, and other emergency exits.
- Invite students to design and produce a scientific catalog of the classroom equipment, including pictures and descriptions of how each item is used.
- Have students research and report on new scientific tools and technology being used throughout the world.
- Invite students to create humorous posters showing how to properly use laboratory and safety equipment.

978-1-4129-5925-4

Name ____ Date ______________

Laboratory Scavenger Hunt

Directions: Place a sticker from each piece of science equipment next to the correct clue. Can you figure out all the clues before time runs out?

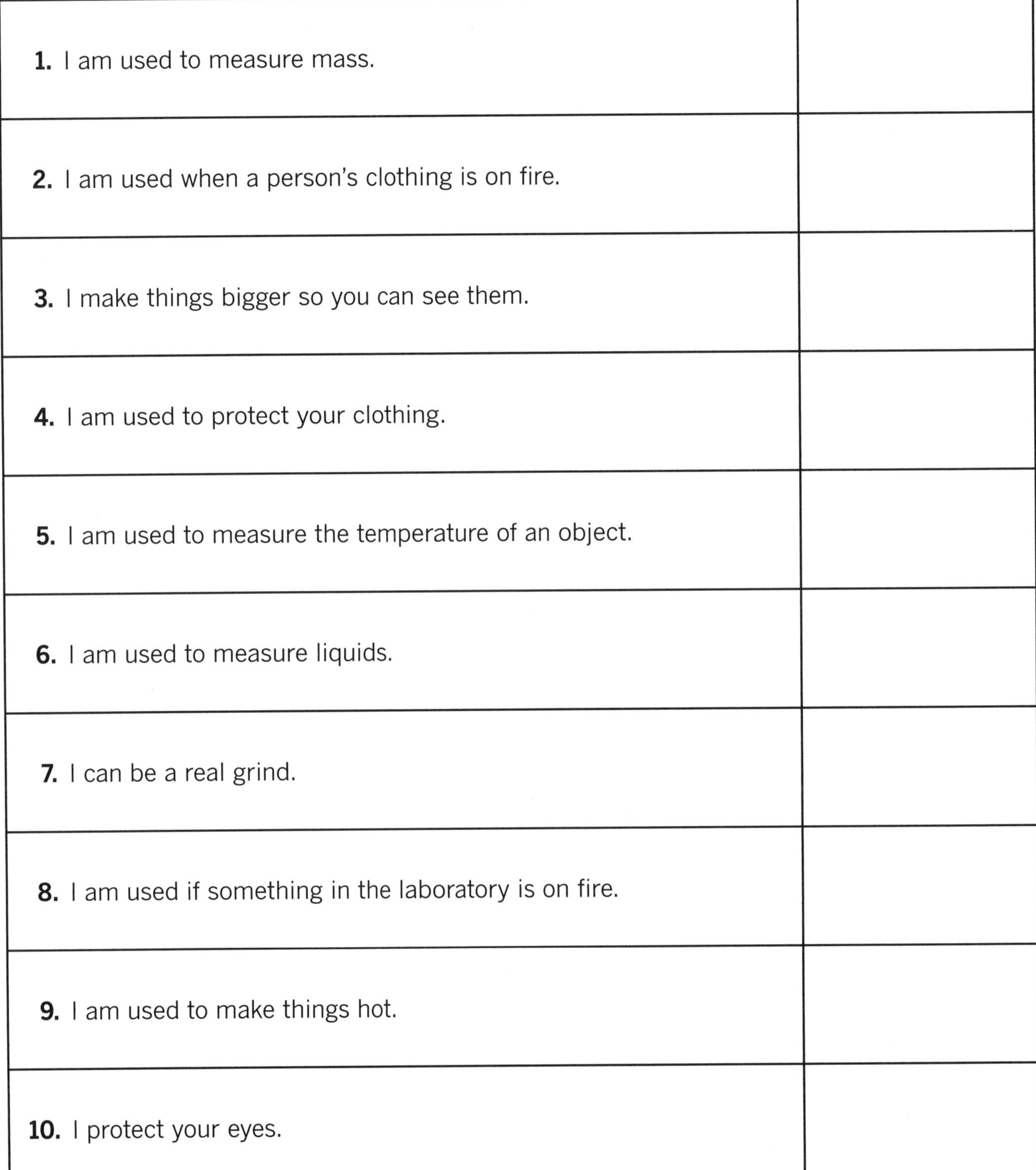

Clue	Sticker
1. I am used to measure mass.	
2. I am used when a person's clothing is on fire.	
3. I make things bigger so you can see them.	
4. I am used to protect your clothing.	
5. I am used to measure the temperature of an object.	
6. I am used to measure liquids.	
7. I can be a real grind.	
8. I am used if something in the laboratory is on fire.	
9. I am used to make things hot.	
10. I protect your eyes.	

Super Scientists

Objectives

Students will learn about the historical contributions of scientists.
Students will identify the roles of different scientists in society.

Many scientists have dedicated their lives to understanding the way our world works. Whether they have questioned certain processes of nature or invented contraptions that advanced society, these scientists have had a major impact on human civilization. In this game, students learn about some of these incredible scientists.

Materials

- Super Scientists Game Cards reproducible
- Super Scientists Spinner reproducible
- cardstock
- scissors
- envelopes
- measuring tools (rulers, compasses)
- large and small flat-end beads (ring and pony beads)
- large brass brads
- art supplies
- chart paper or individual white boards

1. Copy the **Super Scientists Game Cards** and **Super Scientists Spinner reproducibles (pages 13–14)** onto cardstock for each group of three to five students. Cut out the cards and store them in an envelope.
2. Have each group of students make their own "money wheel" spinner as follows. Encourage them to decorate the spinner with science-related artwork.
   a. Label one section of the spinner *Bankrupt*, one *Free Spin*, one *Lose a Turn*, and the rest various amounts of money from *$100* to *$750*.
   b. Cut out the arrow pointer for the spinner. Make a small hole in the center of both the arrow and the circle.
   c. Stack the following parts together, from bottom to top, aligning the holes: cardstock spinner base, large bead, arrow, small bead. Insert a brass brad to connect them together.
   d. Make sure the arrow rotates freely when spun. Adjust the parts as needed.

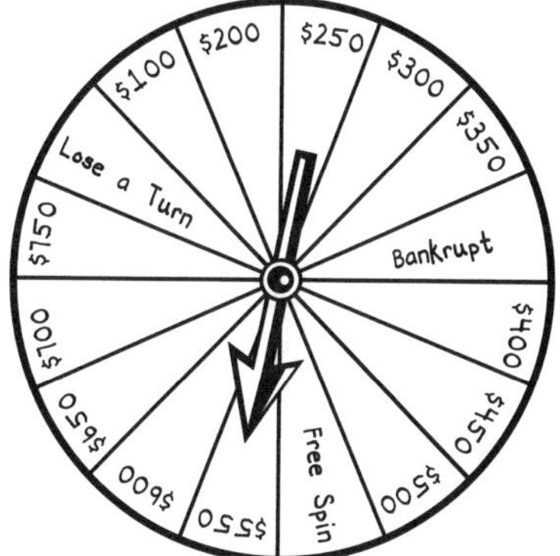

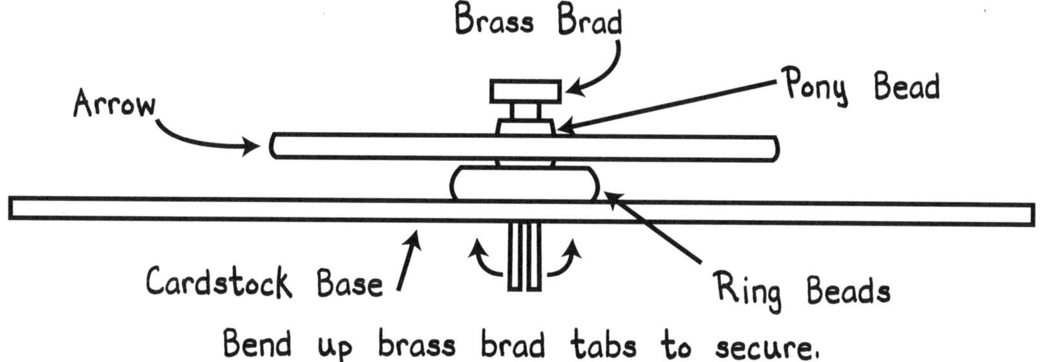

3. Explain to students that the goal of the game is to correctly spell the answer for a given clue, one letter at a time, earning hypothetical money for each correct letter. Demonstrate how to play the game.

a. Read aloud this clue: *I am a scientist who studies plant life.* Draw a row of eight fill-in lines on the board for the letters of the answer. *(botanist)*

b. Players take turns guessing a letter. If correct, write the letter in the appropriate places on the board and record the amount of money earned (for example, $200 per letter). Explain that for the actual game, players spin the money wheel before they guess each letter to determine the letter's value.

c. After each correct guess, players can either guess another letter, or they can guess the entire answer to the clue in the hopes of answering correctly and winning the money. If they answer incorrectly, it's the next player's turn.

d. Continue playing until a player guesses the correct answer. For the actual game, players should continue playing more rounds of fill-in puzzles using the game cards. Explain that players cannot lose any money won during a previous round. They can only lose the money accumulated during the current round. The player with the most money at the end of the game wins.

4. Have each group of students play their own game using their money wheel, a set of game cards, and chart paper (or a white board). For each round, students should rotate the role of "game leader"—the person reading aloud the clues and filling in the letters of the answer—so all students have a chance to earn money. Remind students to spin the money wheel before each new guess. Have them keep score of the money earned after each round for each player. After 30 minutes or after using all of the game cards, the player with the most money wins.

Extended Learning

- Have each group make their own game cards using index cards and facts from their science text and reference materials. Have them trade cards with another group to play the game.
- Ask students to create a booklet or poster about scientists or science careers.
- Invite students to present "A Day in the Life" play about a scientist or science career.
- Have students research one of society's problems (e.g., global warming, hunger, oil shortage) and report on the types of scientists involved in finding the solutions.

978-1-4129-5925-4

Super Scientists Game Cards

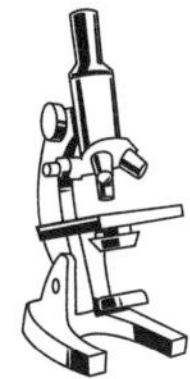

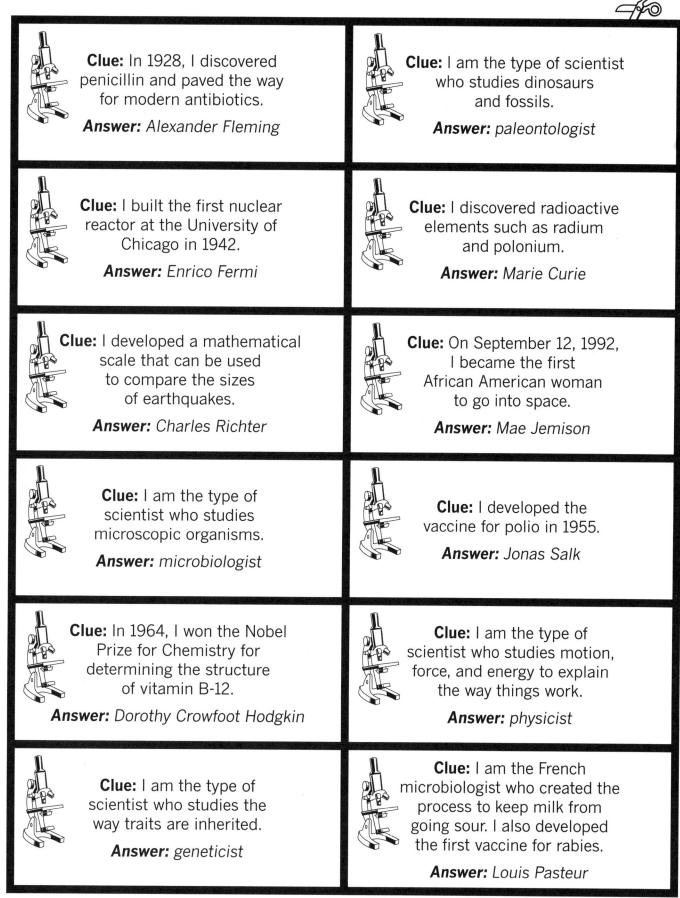

Clue: In 1928, I discovered penicillin and paved the way for modern antibiotics.

Answer: *Alexander Fleming*

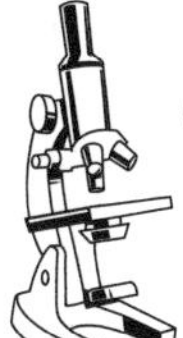

Clue: I am the type of scientist who studies dinosaurs and fossils.

Answer: *paleontologist*

Clue: I built the first nuclear reactor at the University of Chicago in 1942.

Answer: *Enrico Fermi*

Clue: I discovered radioactive elements such as radium and polonium.

Answer: *Marie Curie*

Clue: I developed a mathematical scale that can be used to compare the sizes of earthquakes.

Answer: *Charles Richter*

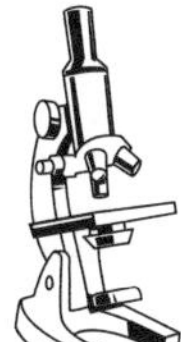

Clue: On September 12, 1992, I became the first African American woman to go into space.

Answer: *Mae Jemison*

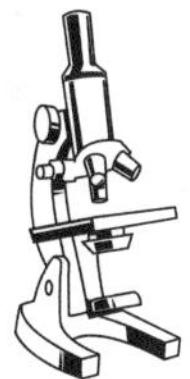

Clue: I am the type of scientist who studies microscopic organisms.

Answer: *microbiologist*

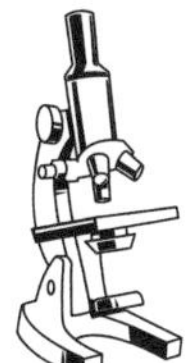

Clue: I developed the vaccine for polio in 1955.

Answer: *Jonas Salk*

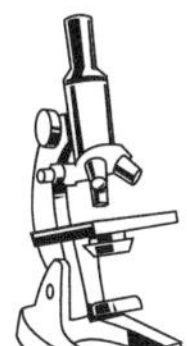

Clue: In 1964, I won the Nobel Prize for Chemistry for determining the structure of vitamin B-12.

Answer: *Dorothy Crowfoot Hodgkin*

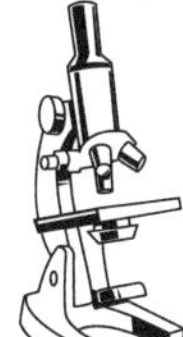

Clue: I am the type of scientist who studies motion, force, and energy to explain the way things work.

Answer: *physicist*

Clue: I am the type of scientist who studies the way traits are inherited.

Answer: *geneticist*

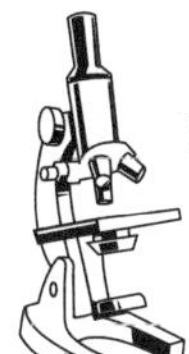

Clue: I am the French microbiologist who created the process to keep milk from going sour. I also developed the first vaccine for rabies.

Answer: *Louis Pasteur*

Super Scientists Spinner

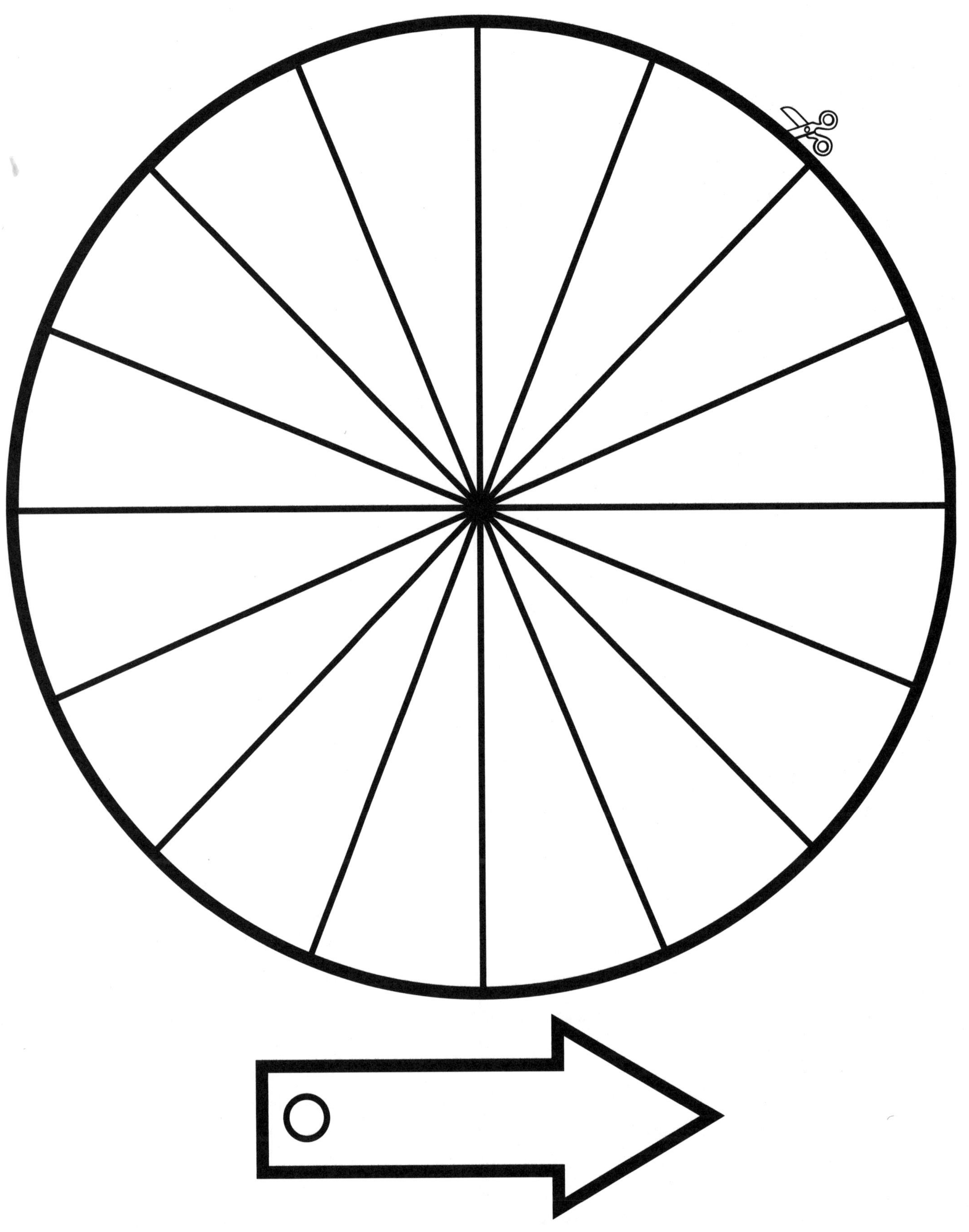

Element Memory Match

Objectives

Students will recognize elements by name and chemical symbol. Students will use the Periodic Table of Elements to identify elements and their symbols.

Memorizing the symbols and names of the periodic elements is important for both chemistry and biology. But the repetitive process of memorization can be unappealing. By turning this task into a game, students will find it easier and motivating to learn the names of the elements and their corresponding symbols.

Materials

- Periodic Table of Elements reproducible
- overhead projector and transparency
- index cards

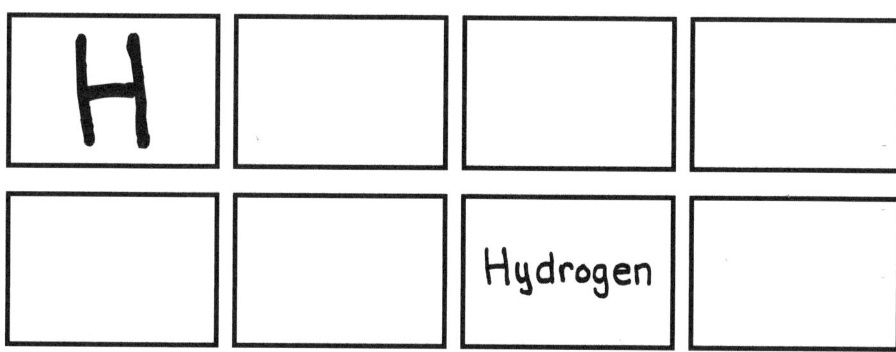

1. Display a transparency of the **Periodic Table of Elements reproducible (page 17)**. Ask students: *What do the letters on the periodic table stand for?* (elements) Tell them that they will play a card game to help them learn the names and symbols of these elements.
2. Assign each pair or trio of students a different family or period of elements (Alkali Metals, Alkaline Earth, Transition Metals, Rare Earth, Other Metals, Metalloids, Non-Metals, Halogens, and Noble Gases). Give them index cards and a copy of the Periodic Table of Elements reproducible. Instruct them to make matching pairs of game cards, writing the element name on one index card and the corresponding symbol for that element on another card.
3. Explain that the object of the game is to find matching pairs of name/symbol cards, similar to the popular game *Concentration*® (a registered trademark of NBC Universal, Inc.).
   a. Players shuffle the cards and place them facedown in rows.
   b. They take turns flipping over any two cards to find a match—an element name and its corresponding symbol.
   c. If they find a match, players get to keep those cards. If they do not, players turn the cards facedown again, and the next player takes a turn.

d. The player with the most matches at the end of the game wins.

4. Demonstrate the game before having students play on their own. Permit players to refer to their Periodic Table of Elements as they play the game for the first time. Then have them replay the game without using the table. Remind students that the game not only challenges them to make matching pairs but also to remember where cards previously turned over are located.

5. Encourage students to trade cards with another group and play the game again using the new deck of elements.

Extended Learning

- Follow-up Element Memory Match with Element Bingo. Use 5 x 5 game cards like those used for Energy Bingo (pages 31–34). Instruct students to write a different element symbol in each space of the game card. Call out element names until someone shouts: *Bingo!*
- Invite students to create and perform a song or a rap about the Periodic Table of Elements.
- Have students draw comic strips or cartoons starring elements as superheroes. Have them include both the name and symbol of the element in their artwork.
- Encourage students to work with a peer drill partner to help them learn the element symbols. Suggest that they practice for five to ten minutes each day until they learn all the elements.

978-1-4129-5925-4

Name ______________________ Date ____________

Periodic Table of Elements

Non-Metals · Alkaline Earth · Transition Metals · Metalloids · Non-Metals · Halogens · Noble Gases · Other Metals · Alkali Metals · Rare Earth

1 **H** Hydrogen																	2 **He** Helium
3 **Li** Lithium	4 **Be** Beryllium											5 **B** Boron	6 **C** Carbon	7 **N** Nitrogen	8 **O** Oxygen	9 **F** Flourine	10 **Ne** Neon
11 **Na** Sodium	12 **Mg** Magnesium											13 **Al** Aluminum	14 **Si** Silicon	15 **P** Phosphorus	16 **S** Sulfur	17 **Cl** Chlorine	18 **Ar** Argon
19 **K** Potassium	20 **Ca** Calcium	21 **Sc** Scandium	22 **Ti** Titanium	23 **V** Vanadium	24 **Cr** Chromium	25 **Mn** Manganese	26 **Fe** Iron	27 **Co** Cobalt	28 **Ni** Nickel	29 **Cu** Copper	30 **Zn** Zinc	31 **Ga** Gallium	32 **Ge** Germanium	33 **As** Arsenic	34 **Se** Selenium	35 **Br** Bromine	36 **Kr** Krypton
37 **Rb** Rubidium	38 **Sr** Strontium	39 **Y** Yttrium	40 **Zr** Zirconium	41 **Nb** Niobium	42 **Mo** Molybdenum	43 **Tc** Technetium	44 **Ru** Ruthenium	45 **Rh** Rhodium	46 **Pd** Palladium	47 **Ag** Silver	48 **Cd** Cadmium	49 **In** Indium	50 **Sn** Tin	51 **Sb** Antimony	52 **Te** Tellurium	53 **I** Iodine	54 **Xe** Xenon
55 **Cs** Cesium	56 **Ba** Barium		72 **Hf** Hafnium	73 **Ta** Tantalum	74 **W** Tungsten	75 **Re** Rhenium	76 **Os** Osmium	77 **Ir** Iridium	78 **Pt** Platinum	79 **Au** Gold	80 **Hg** Mercury	81 **Tl** Thallium	82 **Pb** Lead	83 **Bi** Bismuth	84 **Po** Polonium	85 **At** Astatine	86 **Rn** Radon
87 **Fr** Francium	88 **Ra** Radium		104 **Rf** Rutherfordium	105 **Db** Dubnium	106 **Sg** Seaborgium	107 **Bh** Bohrium	108 **Hs** Hassium	109 **Mt** Meitnerium	110 **Ds** Darmstadtium	111 **Rg** Roentgenium	112 **Uub** Ununbium						

Rare Earth

57 **La** Lanthanum	58 **Ce** Cerium	59 **Pr** Praseodymium	60 **Nd** Neodymium	61 **Pm** Promethium	62 **Sm** Samarium	63 **Eu** Europium	64 **Gd** Gadolinium	65 **Tb** Terbium	66 **Dy** Dysprosium	67 **Ho** Holmium	68 **Er** Erbium	69 **Tm** Thulium	70 **Yb** Ytterbium	71 **Lu** Lutetium
89 **Ac** Actinium	90 **Th** Thorium	91 **Pa** Protactinium	92 **U** Uranium	93 **Np** Neptunium	94 **Pu** Plutonium	95 **Am** Americium	96 **Cm** Curium	97 **Bk** Berkelium	98 **Cf** Californium	99 **Es** Einsteinium	100 **Fm** Fermium	101 **Md** Mendelevium	102 **No** Nobelium	103 **Lr** Lawrencium

Compound Chaos

Materials

- Compound Chaos Game Cards reproducible
- cardstock
- scissors
- index cards
- masking tape
- meter sticks
- pens or markers

Objectives

Students will learn that compounds consist of elements in set ratios. Students will use the Periodic Table of Elements to identify elements in simple compounds.

A chemical compound consists of two or more elements chemically bonded together in a set ratio. A chemical formula is a compact way of writing that relationship, using numbers and symbols to show the amount and type of atoms in each compound. In this hands-on game, students use their whole body to show the correct name and number of atoms used in different chemical compounds.

1. Write the word *salt* on the board. Ask students: *Who knows the chemical name and formula for this common substance?* Write *sodium chloride, NaCl* on the board, pointing out that the chemical name for salt is *sodium chloride,* and the chemical formula is *NaCl.* Ask: *How many atoms of sodium and chlorine are in one molecule of sodium chloride?* (one atom of each element)
2. Explain to students that they will play a game of Compound Chaos to help them learn the formulas of some common compounds, such as NaCl. Give each group of four to six students the **Compound Chaos Game Cards reproducible (page 20)** copied onto cardstock and cut out for the game. Ask students: *What are the eight elements used in these compounds?* (sodium, chlorine, calcium, potassium, oxygen, hydrogen, bromine, sulfur)
3. Take students to an outdoor play area or have them push back their desks in the classroom. Give each group masking tape and a meter stick to make a vertical rectangle on the floor measuring one meter by two meters. Have them use tape to divide the rectangle into a 4 x 6 grid (24 squares in all).
4. To complete their rectangular game board, have students write each of the following names three times on separate strips of masking tape (one name per strip) and randomly stick the 24 strips in separate squares of the grid: *sodium, chlorine, calcium, potassium, oxygen, hydrogen, bromine, sulfur*.
5. To start the game, one student selects a game card and uses his or her hands and feet on the game board to show the correct ratio of elements in the compound. For example, if the compound is $CaCl_2$, he or she can place one hand and two feet (or two hands and one foot) on one *calcium* square and two *chlorine* squares.

 978-1-4129-5925-4

6. While the first player maintains position on the game board, the next player takes a turn, choosing a card and using his or her hands and feet to show the correct formula.
7. After all players have taken a turn, and if they are all still in position on the game board, the first player starts again, taking another card to show on the game board.
8. The game continues until a player falls or until there are no longer enough spaces for another student to show a compound. Any player still in position earns one point.
9. Have students clear the game board and play another round. The game continues until a player reaches a total of 15 points and wins the game.

Extended Learning

- Encourage students to use index cards to make more game cards using other compounds, modifying the game board as needed to play the new game.
- Have students list chemical compounds written on food and drink labels from their lunch. Encourage them to use those compounds to make more game cards.
- Have students use the Periodic Table of Elements reproducible (page 17) to identify any patterns of compounds used in the game.

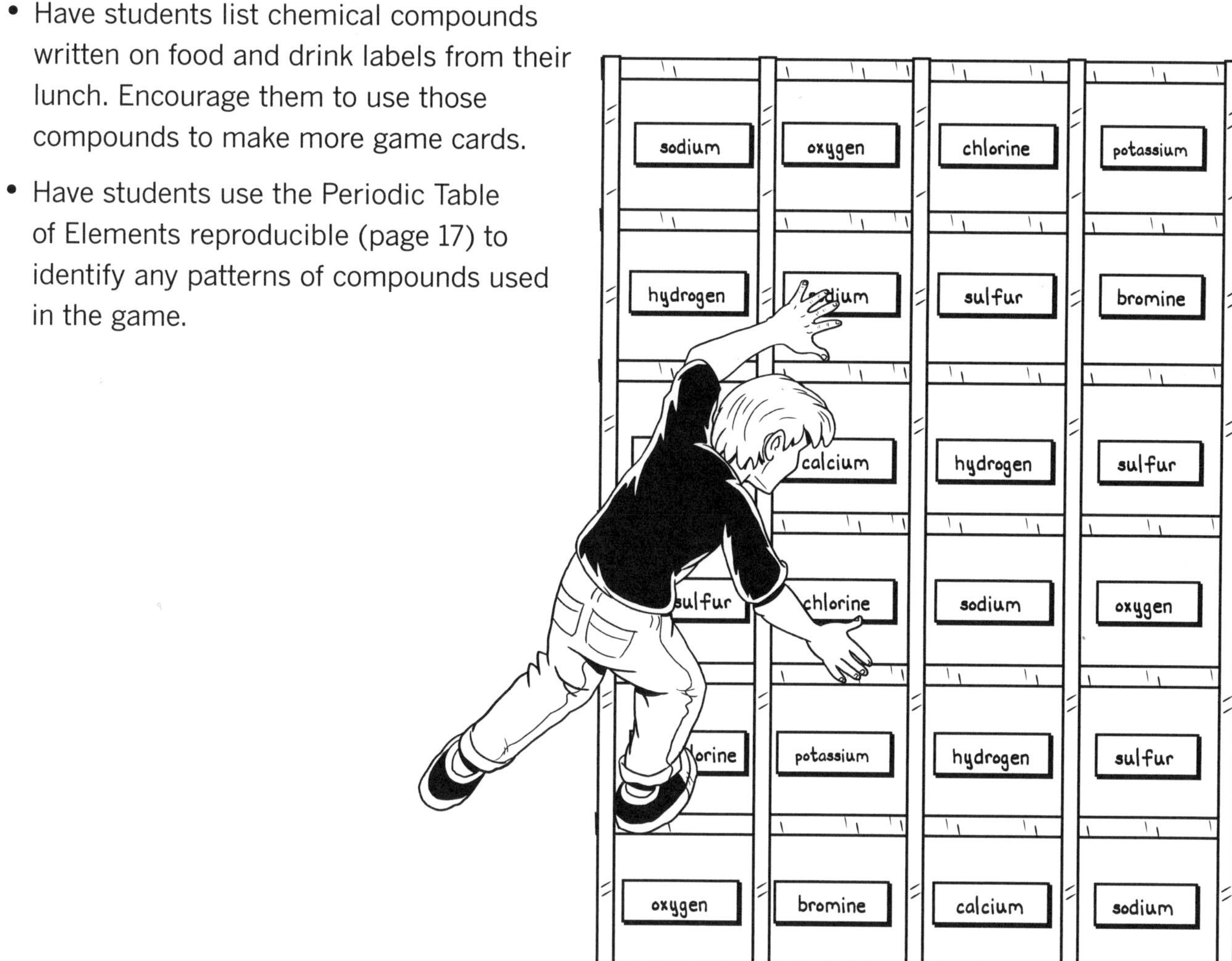

978-1-4129-5925-4

Compound Chaos Game Cards

NaCl	H_2O	$CaCl_2$
KBr	K_2O	$CaBr_2$
Na_2O	Na_2S	HCl
HBr	CaS	K_2S

978-1-4129-5925-4 • © Corwin Press

Shuffleboard Showdown

Objectives

Students will investigate the relationship between force and motion. Students will experiment with acceleration and energy transfer.

According to Newton's Laws, an object at rest tends to stay at rest, and an object in motion tends to stay in motion with the same speed and in the same direction, unless acted upon by an unbalanced force. In this game, students learn how to modify and adjust their use of force and motion to outscore their opponent. They also observe how energy is transferred when objects collide during the game.

Materials

- masking tape
- red and black checkers
- scrap paper for scorekeeping

1. Review Newton's Laws of Motion with students. Ask: *What makes things move?* (any force such as pushing, pulling, throwing, dropping) Invite students to describe different forces they use every day. Then tell them that they will be using their knowledge of force and motion to play a game of Shuffleboard Showdown.
2. Assign each pair of students a long play area for the game, such as a long table, lab bench, or area on the floor. Have them use masking tape to make a shuffleboard triangle like the one shown above. If the game area is on the floor, have them also designate a starting line. Give student pairs six checkers (three red checkers for one player and three black checkers for the other).
3. To play the game, players use a pencil to push each of their three checkers the length of the play area and into the triangular scoreboard. The challenge is to use just the right amount of force and direction to propel the checkers into the sections that have the greatest point values. Players may also try to knock their opponent's checkers out of the high-scoring areas.

4. After all six checkers have been used, players total the scores and clear the board for another round. The first player to accumulate 50 points wins the game.
5. After the game, invite students to share their strategies for getting the highest score. Encourage them to share their results and suggest ways to improve the game.

Extended Learning

- Invite students to make a different scoreboard for the game by changing the shape, size, or values of the sections.
- Have students use a stopwatch and measuring tape to measure both the duration and the distance of each propelled checker during the game. Then have them calculate the speed by dividing distance by time. Encourage them to make generalizations about their results, including which speed worked best.
- Have students define and illustrate the words *force, speed, inertia, friction, gravity, acceleration,* and *momentum.*
- Challenge students to think of other games that utilize and teach about force and motion.

1
1
Speed: The rate or a measure of the rate of motion.

 978-1-4129-5925-4

Phase Change Card Game

Objective

Students will learn that increasing or decreasing kinetic energy or heat can cause a change in the state of matter (solid, liquid, gas, plasma).

Materials
- index cards

Matter exists in four different states: solid, liquid, gas, and plasma (ionized gas). The physical characteristics of each state, such as shape and volume, are determined by the kinetic energy and attractive forces of the molecules. In this game, students learn how kinetic energy can affect the state of matter.

1. Review the four different states of matter with students. Ask: *What is solid water called?* (ice) *What must happen to make ice change to liquid water?* (heat the ice to make it melt) Explain that when heat is added, the kinetic energy of the water molecules increases, causing the water to change from one state to another.
2. Give each group of two to four students a set of 50 index cards and have them make five copies of each of these terms: *increase in kinetic energy, decrease in kinetic energy, increase in heat, decrease in heat, solid, liquid, gas, ice, water, steam.*
3. Explain that the object of the game is to collect sets of three cards that describe a change in kinetic energy or heat and the corresponding phase changes. With a volunteer, model and explain how to play the game:
   a. To begin the game, the dealer deals five cards to each player and then places the remaining cards facedown in a reserve pile.
   b. Players start their turn by either putting down a set of three matching cards faceup on the table, such as *liquid, increase in kinetic energy,* and *gas*, or choosing a card from the reserve pile to try to complete a matching set.
   c. After they put down each set, players get to draw another card from the reserve pile to try to complete another set. If that is not possible, the next player takes a turn.
   d. The game continues until one player runs out of cards or there are no more cards in the reserve pile. The player with the most sets of cards on the table wins.

4. After students finish playing the game, have them write five of their winning combinations. Ask them to predict what would happen if the energy changes in their winning combinations were reversed.

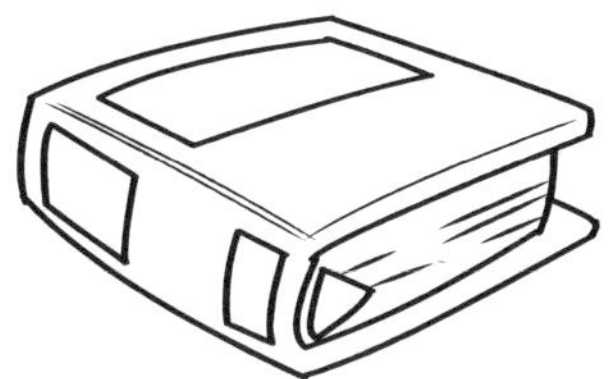

Extended Learning

- Have students make a new sets of game cards using phase changes for other substances.
- Have students research the water cycle and write a humorous, fictional story about the travels of a raindrop through the water cycle.
- Have students role-play different states of matter.
- Invite an expert from the physics or engineering department of a local university to speak about cryobiology, cryogenics, or cryopreservation of human tissue.

978-1-4129-5925-4

Atomic Marble Madness

Objectives

Students will read and interpret a Periodic Table of Elements.
Students will describe atomic parts and make models of electron configurations.

Atomic models often give beginning chemistry students the incorrect impression that electrons move in fixed orbits around the nucleus of an atom. In this game, students use an array of marbles to represent the movement of electrons in electron clouds. They will place the correct number of subatomic particles in the proper position of an electron configuration to show a more realistic view of an atom.

1. Invite students to share what they know about atoms. Ask: *What are the basic building blocks of all matter?* (atoms) *What are the three main particles of an atom?* (protons, neutrons, electrons) *Where are the protons and neutrons located in an atom?* (in the nucleus) *Where are the electrons located?* (outside the nucleus) *How do you know the number of protons, electrons, and neutrons in an atom?* (atomic number = number of protons = number of electrons in a neutral atom; atomic mass number of protons + number of neutrons)
2. Explain to students that the electrons of an atom move in different energy levels around the nucleus, moving continuously and rapidly in a cloudlike blur. The first energy level (closest to the nucleus) can hold two electrons, the second energy level can hold the next eight electrons, and the third energy level can hold up to 18 more electrons. Each energy level, or shell, can hold up to $2n^2$ electrons, where n equals the shell number. Ask: *How do you know the number of electrons in a neutral atom?* (It's the same as the number of protons, or the atomic number.)
3. Give students two sheets of poster board, a compass, a ruler, and scissors to make their own individual game boards, as follows:
   a. Draw on one sheet of poster board four circles inside of each other like a target. Make the center circle at least three inches in diameter, and leave about one and one-half inches of space between the circles.
   b. Inside the center circle, write *N* for *nucleus*.
   c. Inside the spaces between the remaining circles, write *1, 2,* and *3* from the center outward to represent the circular pathways of the first three energy levels.

Materials

- Atomic Marble Madness Game Cards reproducible
- Periodic Table of Elements reproducible
- poster board
- compasses
- rulers
- scissors
- tape
- 2 colors of small marbles or cereal balls
- bowls
- index cards

d. Cut two-inch-wide strips from the second sheet of poster board to make circles the exact same size as the circles drawn on the first sheet. Tape the strips of poster board around the corresponding drawn circles to create railings for marbles.

4. Give each group of three to five students two bowls of different-colored marbles (or cereal balls). One color represents protons, and the other color represents electrons. Have them write on separate index cards the symbols of elements with atomic numbers 18 or less. Have them also use index cards to make game cards like those on the **Atomic Marble Madness Game Cards reproducible (page 28)**. Have them cut out and glue the boxes to index cards to begin their card set. Each group should make at least 50 game cards. Provide groups with a Periodic Table of Elements reproducible (page 17) to use as a reference.

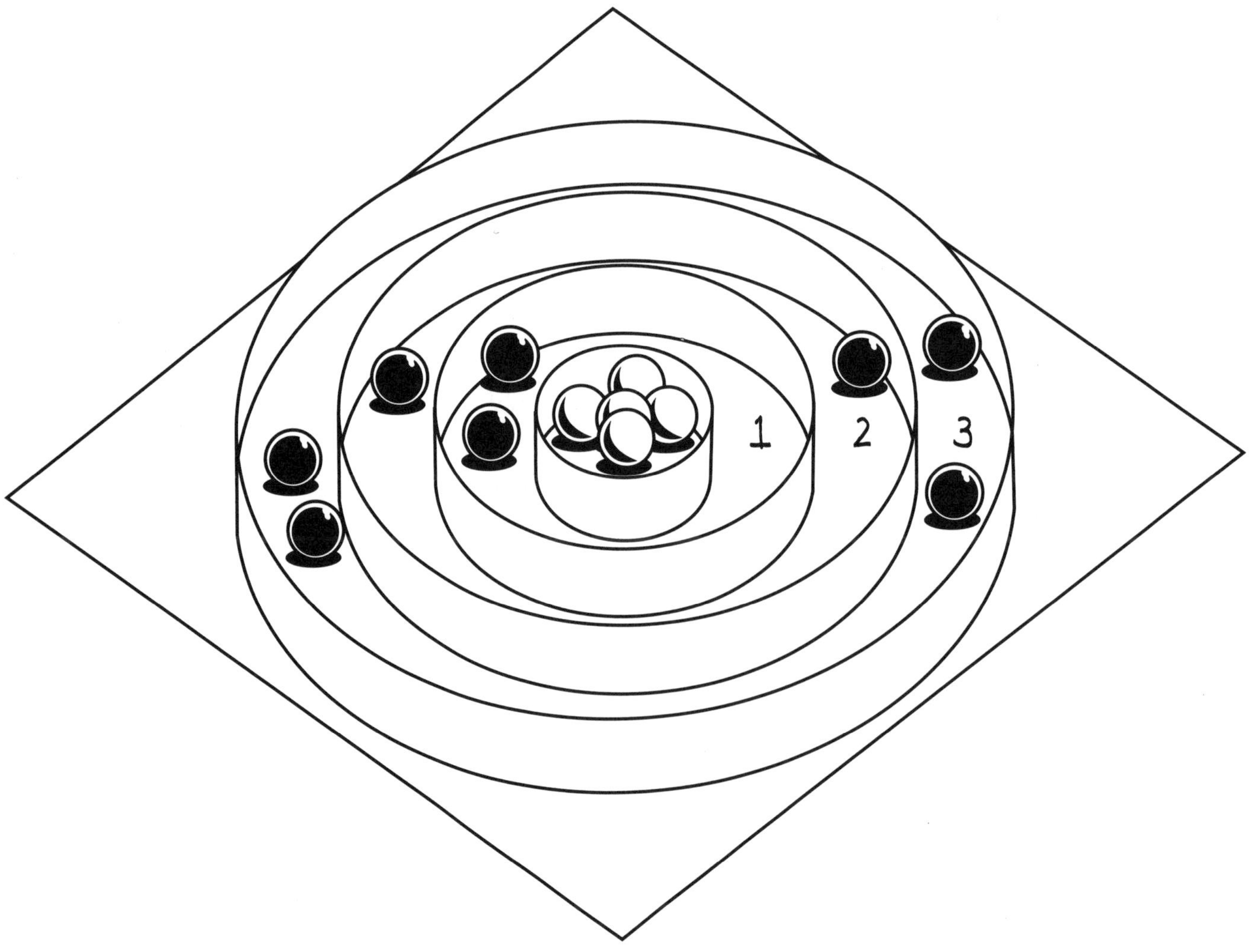

5. After groups have constructed their game boards and completed their game cards, model and explain the rules of the game:
   a. To begin, each group chooses an element card as their target element. The object of the game is to be the first player to complete a marble model of the electron configuration of that neutral atom, including both protons and electrons.
   b. Players earn marbles by correctly answering the game cards.
   c. The first player reads a game-card question to an opponent. If the opponent answers correctly, he or she earns a marble. If not, the first player earns the marble.
   d. Players put each "proton" marble inside the center circle (nucleus) of their game board and each "electron" marble, sequentially, in the energy levels marked *1, 2* and *3,* filling them from lowest to highest level (e.g., 2*e*, 8*e*, 18*e*).
   e. Players continue taking turns selecting game cards and reading them aloud to different opponents. The first player to complete his or her atomic model wins.

6. Encourage students to refer to the Periodic Table of Elements as they play the game. Have groups exchange game cards to play more rounds of the game.

7. As a follow-up, invite students to draw or make models of the elements they created on the game board.

Extended Learning

Use the game cards to play Atomic Musical Chairs with the class. Set up a row of chairs for all but one student. Play fast-paced music as students walk around the chairs. When you stop the music, students must sit in a chair. The student left standing must answer a question to stay in the game. Remove a chair after each elimination. The last player sitting wins the game.

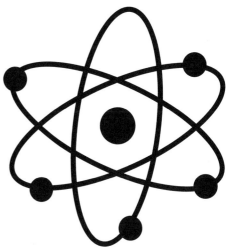

Atomic Marble Madness Game Cards

Question: How many protons does a magnesium atom have?

Answer: *12 protons*

Question: How many electrons does a neon atom have?

Answer: *10 electrons*

Question: What are the three basic subatomic particles?

Answer: *protons, neutrons, electrons*

Question: An element is determined by the number of ______.

Answer: *protons*

Question: Which subatomic particles are found in the nucleus of an atom?

Answer: *protons and neutrons*

Question: What is the electrical charge of a proton?

Answer: *positive*

Question: What is the electrical charge of a neutron?

Answer: *none, neutrons are neutral*

Question: What is the electrical charge of an electron?

Answer: *negative*

Question: What is the electrical charge of an atom's nucleus?

Answer: *positive*

Question: What is the electrical charge of an atom?

Answer: *none, atoms are neutral*

Question: How many electrons can fit in the first energy level (orbital) surrounding the nucleus of an atom?

Answer: *two electrons*

Question: How many total electrons fill the first three energy levels (orbitals) surrounding the nucleus of an atom?

Answer: *28 electrons*

Chain Reaction Contraption

Objectives

Students will identify, describe, and compare simple machines. Students will use their knowledge of simple machines to construct a complex machine.

There are six types of simple machines—pulley, lever, inclined plane, wheel and axle, wedge, and screw. Simple machines make work easier by increasing, decreasing, or changing the direction of force. In this game, students use their knowledge of simple machines to build a contraption that "traps" their opponent.

1. Begin by displaying examples of the six simple machines and asking students questions about them. For example, display a wheel and axle, and ask: *Where have you seen this kind of simple machine?* (Possible answer: *on a car*) Tell students that they will use their knowledge of simple machines to build a contraption for a game.
2. Give each group of four or five students a sheet of poster board to create a game board consisting of a twisted pathway of at least 30 spaces. The spaces should include the labels *Start, Lose a Turn, Go Back to Start, End, Go Back 2 Spaces,* and five *Trapped!* spaces. Encourage students to decorate their game board with pictures of simple machines.
3. Tell students that the object of the game is to build a complex contraption to trap each opponent's game piece on one of the *Trapped!* spaces. Their contraption should consist of at least three simple machines working in a chain reaction to drop a trap onto the game board. They may only touch their contraption once to start the chain reaction. Display and review the following example before having students build their own. Invite students to identify each simple machine used.

Chain Reaction Contraption

A marble slides down a marble track and lands in a cup. The cup drops and knocks down a row of dominoes, which hits a baseball and starts it rolling. The baseball rolls down a ramp and hits a water bottle. The water bottle empties into a funnel and fills a cup on a string. The cup falls, unwinding the string attached to a pulley, which causes an inverted cup to drop onto the game board, trapping the game piece.

Materials

- examples or pictures of simple machines (pulley, lever, inclined plane, wheel and axle, wedge, screw)
- poster board
- art supplies
- supplies to create contraptions (e.g., cardboard strips, paper cups, tape, screws string, dominoes, rulers, dowels, marbles, ball bearings, coins, paper clips)
- sticky notes
- colored counters or other game pieces
- dice

4. After they complete their game board, all players put their game piece on *Start*. Players also each claim a different *Trapped!* space on the game board, putting their name on it using a sticky note. To play the game, players take turns rolling the dice and moving that number of spaces on the board. If a player lands on a *Trapped!* space, the student whose name is on the space sets up his or her contraption and tries to capture the player's game piece. If successful, the game piece's owner is out of the game. The player with the greatest number of captured game pieces wins the game.
5. After they finish playing the game, invite students to summarize how well their contraption worked and how they might improve it. Have them draw a picture of their contraption and label all of the simple machines they used.

Extended Learning

- Have students revise their contraption and play the game again.
- Invite students to make a class book titled *The ABCs of Simple Machines* and include drawings or pictures of simple machines.
- Encourage students to investigate Rube Goldberg machines—complex machines designed to perform simple tasks in entertaining, roundabout ways. Assign a simple task, such as turning on a lightbulb or popping a balloon, and challenge students to think of an entertaining, complex contraption to perform the task.

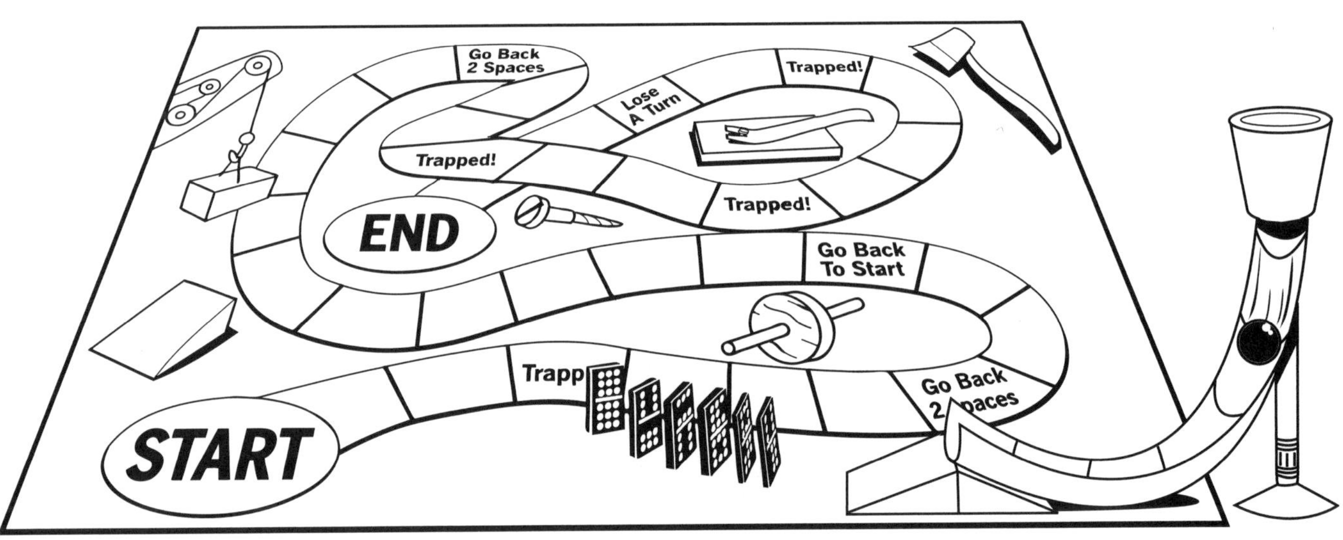

 978-1-4129-5925-4

Energy Bingo

Objective

Students will identify and define energy vocabulary.

Energy is the ability to do work. There are many forms of energy, including electrical, mechanical, thermal, and chemical. In this game, students review different energy vocabulary by playing a scientific version of the game *Bingo*.

Materials

- Energy Vocabulary Cards reproducible
- Bingo Game Card reproducible
- index cards
- counters, paper squares, or other game markers

1. Introduce the topic of energy by listing different types of energy on the board and inviting students to describe how people use energy every day. For example:
   - thermal *(heating homes, cooking food)*
   - mechanical *(riding a bicycle, using machines to move objects)*
   - electrical *(lighting homes, playing video games, watching TV)*
   - chemical *(combustion in car engines, batteries)*
   - radiant *(solar cells, solar heat)*
   - nuclear *(power plants)*
2. Display the following list of vocabulary terms (or use your own list) and assign one or two terms to each student. Have students make a game card for each of their assigned terms by writing a clue about it and the answer on an index card, as shown on the **Energy Vocabulary Cards reproducible (page 33)**. Give students a copy of the reproducible to use as a reference. The clues can be either a definition or an example of how that item is used.

Energy Vocabulary

chemical energy
combustion
conduction
convection
elastic potential energy
electrical energy
electricity
electromagnetic energy
energy
fossil fuels
freezing point
gravitational potential energy
heat
heat engine
insulator
Kelvin scale
kinetic energy
law of conservation of energy
mechanical energy
melting point
nuclear energy
potential energy
power
power plant
radiant energy
radiation
solar energy
specific heat
thermal energy
thermal expansion
vaporization
work

3. Give students a copy of the **Bingo Game Card reproducible (page 34)** and tell them to choose 24 vocabulary terms from the list and write them randomly in separate sections of the game card.

4. To play the game, select and read aloud the vocabulary clues to the class as students use counters (or other markers) to cover the corresponding answers on their game card. When students get five in a row, either horizontally, vertically, or diagonally, they should shout: *Bingo!* Ask them to read aloud their answers for you to check. The first student to get five correct answers in a row wins the game.

5. Repeat the game several times, inviting volunteers to select and read aloud the clues.

Extended Learning

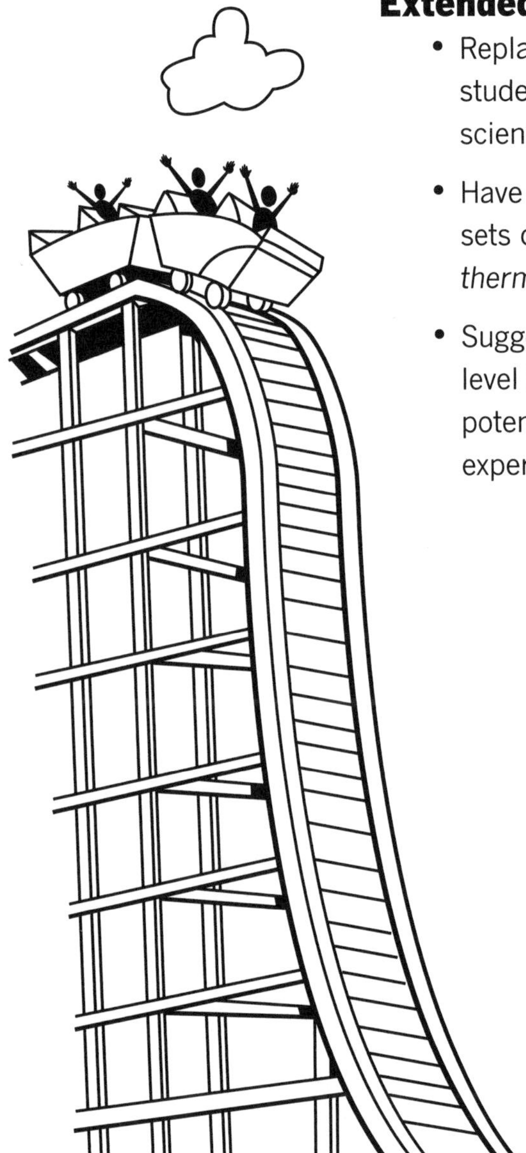

- Replay the game using another set of game cards written by students. Have them include vocabulary terms about other science concepts.
- Have students create and complete analogies to show how two sets of concepts are related. For example, *radiant energy: light :: thermal energy:* ______. (heat)
- Suggest that students create and present an elementary-level lesson about the difference between kinetic energy and potential energy. Encourage them to include visuals and a simple experiment in their lesson.

978-1-4129-5925-4

Name ______________________ Date ____________

Energy Vocabulary Cards

Clue: Ability to do work

Answer: *energy*

Clue: Energy of motion

Answer: *kinetic energy*

Clue: Stored energy

Answer: *potential energy*

Clue: Energy from the sun

Answer: *solar energy*

Clue: Light

Answer: *radiant energy*

Clue: Heat

Answer: *thermal energy*

Clue: Energy transferred directly from one object to another

Answer: *conduction*

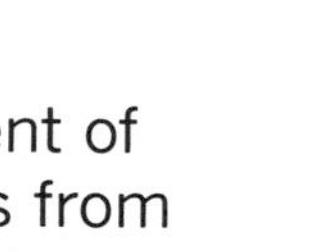

Clue: Movement of liquids or gases from a cooler area to a warmer area

Answer: *convection*

Clue: Movement of electrons

Answer: *electricity*

Name ______________________________ Date ______________

Bingo Game Card

Directions: Write a different vocabulary term in each box. Listen to the clues and use markers to cover terms that match the clues. If you cover five in a row, shout: *Bingo!*

		FREE SPACE		

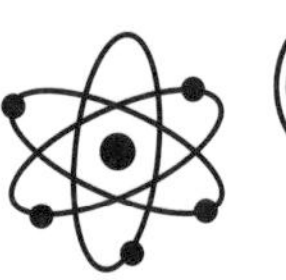

978-1-4129-5925-4 • © Corwin Press

Energy Hot Potato

Objectives

Students will explore and discuss ways to conserve energy.
Students will identify, describe, and compare different types of energy, including renewable and nonrenewable resources.

Playing a game while reviewing lesson concepts can greatly increase students' retention of the material. In this game, students review the "hot" topic of energy conservation, including types of energy, how they are obtained, how they are distributed, and alternate forms of energy.

Materials

- Energy Hot Potato Game Cards reproducible
- scissors
- index cards
- beanbag or other soft object
- science reference materials

1. Photocopy and cut out the game cards on the **Energy Hot Potato Game Cards reproducible (page 37)**. You may also make additional game cards by writing your own questions and answers on index cards.
2. Display the following passage about fossil fuels and read it aloud to students:

> **Did You Know?**
> There are three main forms of fossil fuels: oil, coal, and natural gas. Fossil fuels take millions of years to form. The fossil fuels we use today were formed hundreds of millions of years ago, before the age of the dinosaurs. Fossil fuels are *nonrenewable* forms of energy—once they are gone, they are gone. We can save fossil fuels by conserving energy and using alternative forms of energy that are renewable, such as solar, wind, biomass, hydropower, or geothermal energy.

3. Ask students to brainstorm ways to conserve energy as you list their ideas on the board. Ask: *How can we conserve energy?* (Possible answers: *turn off lights when you leave a room, recycle, combine errands*) *What other sources of energy can be used other than fossil fuels?* (Possible answers: *solar, wind, hydroelectric*) Point out that energy sources such as solar and wind power are *renewable*—they are inexhaustible sources of energy that can be replenished in a short period of time.
4. Invite students to stand in a large circle to play a game of Energy Hot Potato. Begin the game by tossing a beanbag (or other soft object) to a student and reading aloud a question from one of the game cards. The student must answer the question quickly and correctly and then toss the beanbag to another student who must answer the next question you read aloud. If a student does not

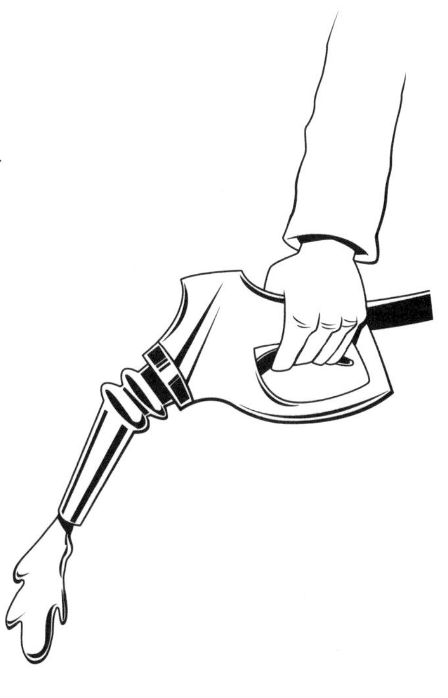

answer the question correctly or drops the beanbag, he or she is out of the game. The last student remaining in the game wins.

5. As a follow-up, ask students to make more game cards to play the game again. Encourage them to use facts from their science textbooks or from other science reference materials.

Extended Learning

- Invite an expert to speak to the class about renewable and nonrenewable energy resources. You might also arrange for a class trip to a local hydroelectric plant.
- Assign students to a form of energy and have them research and prepare a presentation about it. Have them include where the energy comes from, how it gets converted into useable energy, the pros and cons of using that energy source, and its effects on the environment.
- Invite students to make an energy picture book that includes both drawings and factual information about different types of energy.

978-1-4129-5925-4

Energy Hot Potato Game Cards

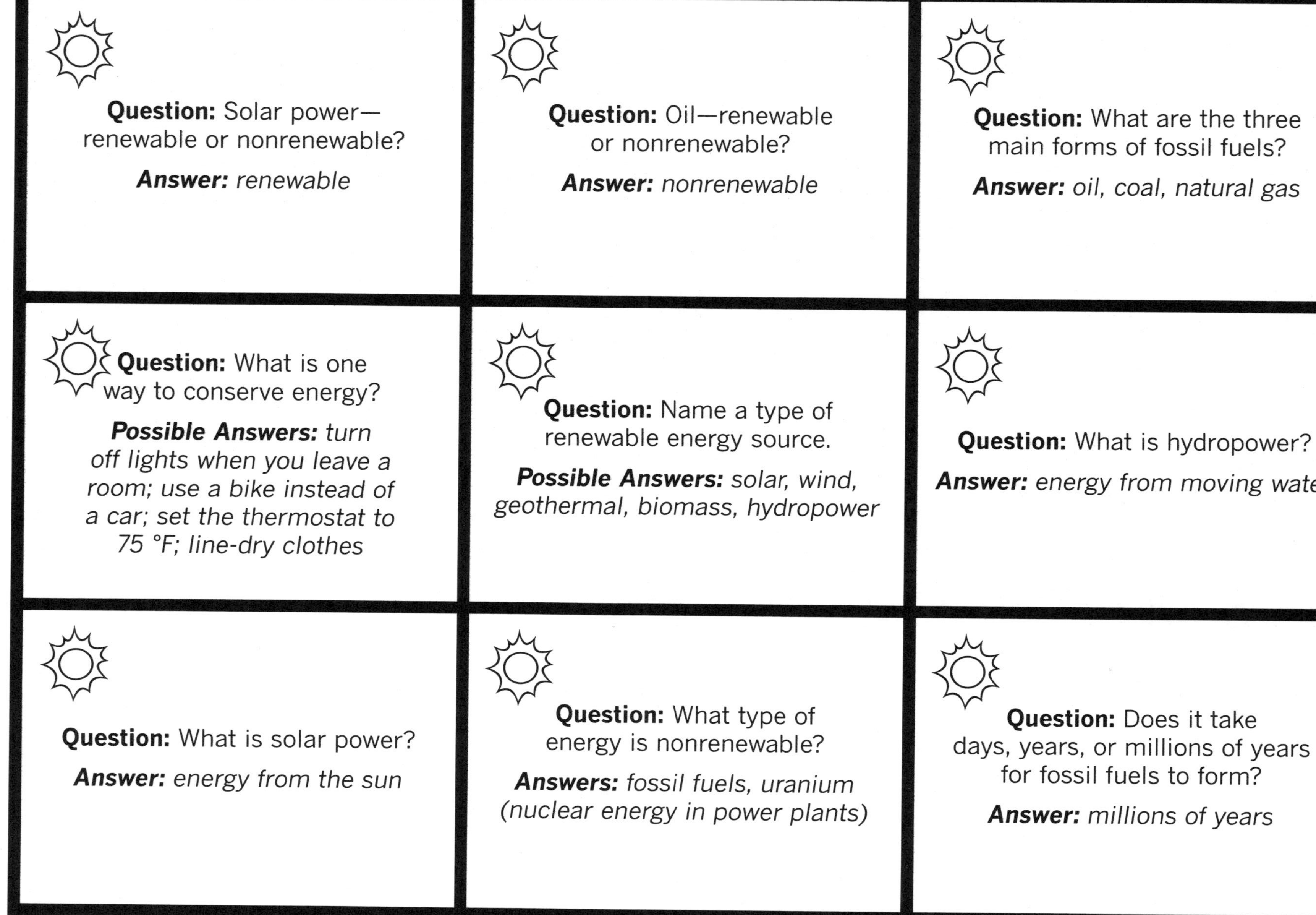

Question: Solar power—renewable or nonrenewable?

Answer: *renewable*

Question: Oil—renewable or nonrenewable?

Answer: *nonrenewable*

Question: What are the three main forms of fossil fuels?

Answer: *oil, coal, natural gas*

Question: What is one way to conserve energy?

Possible Answers: *turn off lights when you leave a room; use a bike instead of a car; set the thermostat to 75 °F; line-dry clothes*

Question: Name a type of renewable energy source.

Possible Answers: *solar, wind, geothermal, biomass, hydropower*

Question: What is hydropower?

Answer: *energy from moving water*

Question: What is solar power?

Answer: *energy from the sun*

Question: What type of energy is nonrenewable?

Answers: *fossil fuels, uranium (nuclear energy in power plants)*

Question: Does it take days, years, or millions of years for fossil fuels to form?

Answer: *millions of years*

CHAPTER 2

Life Science

Crafty Cells

Materials

- Crafty Cells reproducible
- diagram of a plant cell and an animal cell
- poster board
- containers of assorted craft supplies (pipe cleaners, ribbon, yarn, assorted beads, small seeds, clay, foam peanuts, foam balls, cellophane, colored tissue)
- glue and tape
- reward tokens or treats
- reference materials about cells (optional)

Objectives

Students will distinguish between plant cells and animal cells. Students will identify, describe, and compare cell parts and their functions.

In the 1660s, Robert Hook discovered the *cell*—the smallest unit of life—by observing the composition of cork cells under a simple microscope. Because the microscopic structure reminded him of a monk's room, which was called a *cellula,* Hook decided to call the structures *cells*. In this game, students create and use artistic models to identify and compare the parts of a cell.

1. Display a diagram of a plant cell and an animal cell for students to compare and contrast. Ask: *What differences do you see between these two cells?* (Possible answer: *Plant cells have a cell wall, chloroplasts, and a large vacuole that animal cells do not have.*) Point out some of the organelles and discuss their functions.

Organelle	Function
Cell wall	Enclosure that gives plant cells structure and support
Chloroplast	Organelle where photosynthesis takes place in green plants
Golgi body	Packages macromolecules for transport
Mitochondrion	Cell's "power plant"
Nucleus	Cell's "control center"
Ribosome	Organelle that synthesizes protein
Rough ER	Endoplasmic reticulum where ribosomes are produced
Smooth ER	Transfers proteins to other locations; has no ribosomes

2. Divide the class into small groups. Give each group a sheet of poster board, a container of craft supplies, and a copy of the

978-1-4129-5925-4

Crafty Cells reproducible (page 40). Give them 20 minutes to make an artistic but accurate representation of a plant cell or an animal cell. Instruct them to select craft items that best represent each part of the cell (e.g., twisted pipe cleaners for DNA, tiny beads for ribosomes).

3. Then play a game of Crafty Cells, in which each group shows their completed artwork to the class. Invite classmates to guess the organelle represented by each craft item. Reward correct answers with tokens or treats.

4. After the game, display the completed artwork around the room for students to compare and contrast. You might also suggest that students research and write information cards to accompany their cell models.

Extended Learning

- Have students work in cooperative groups to write a children's book about a cell. Tell them to include an introduction to the cell and how it was discovered, a comparison between plant and animal cells, and the function of each organelle.

- Invite students to write cinquain poems about different organelles. Remind them that a *cinquain* is a five-line poem using the following format: one word, two descriptive words, three action words, a four-word phrase, and one word that is a synonym of the first word. Bind the poems together to make a class book.

Cross Section of a Plant Cell

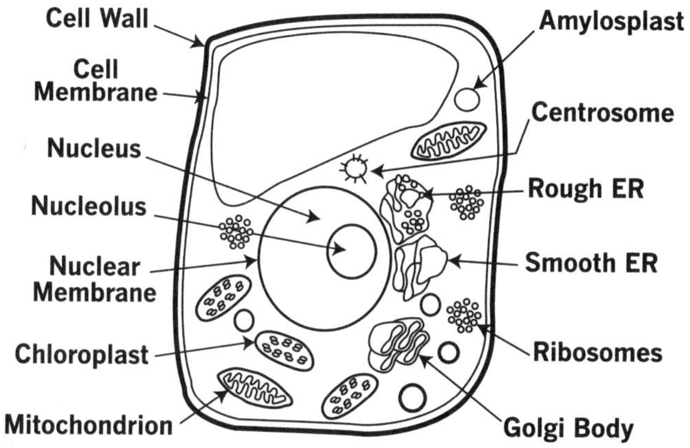

Cross Section of an Animal Cell

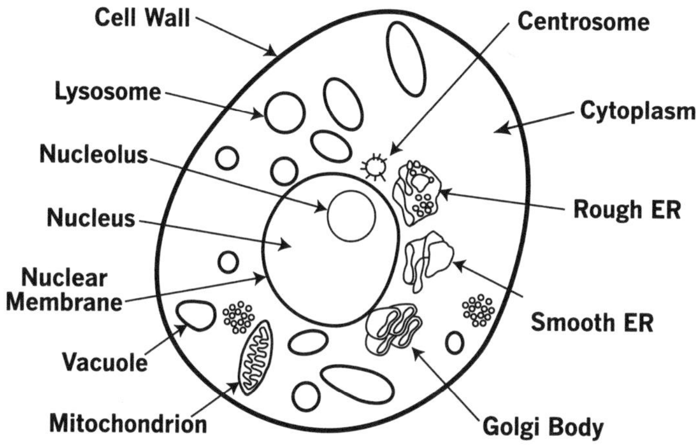

Name ______________________ Date ______________

Crafty Cells

Directions: Make an artistic but accurate representation of a plant cell or an animal cell. List the craft items used.

Kind of Cell: ______________________

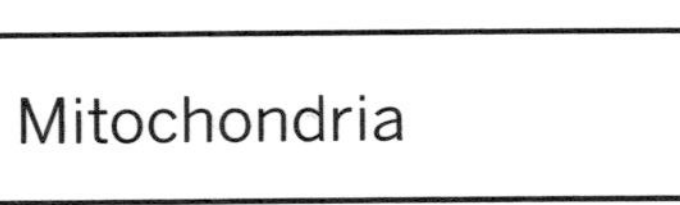
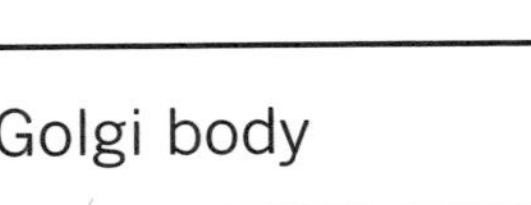
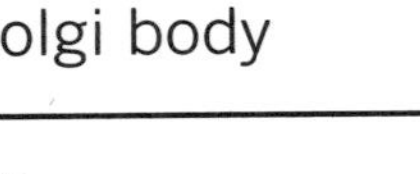
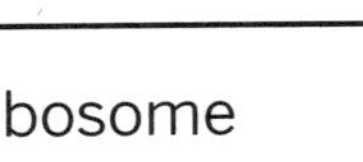
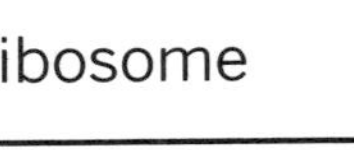
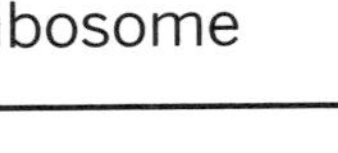
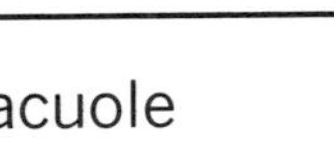
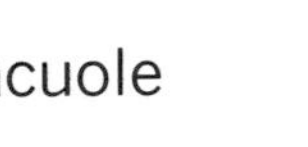
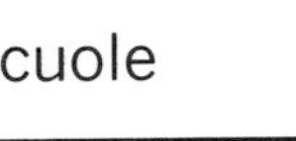
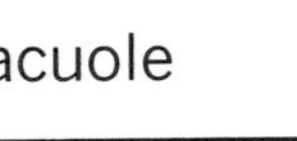
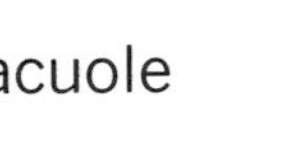
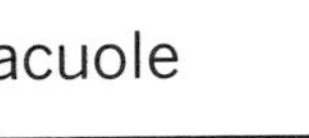
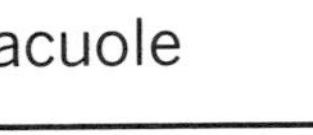
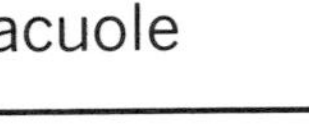
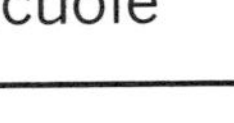
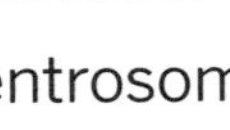
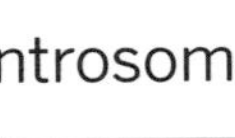
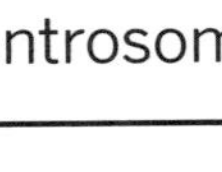

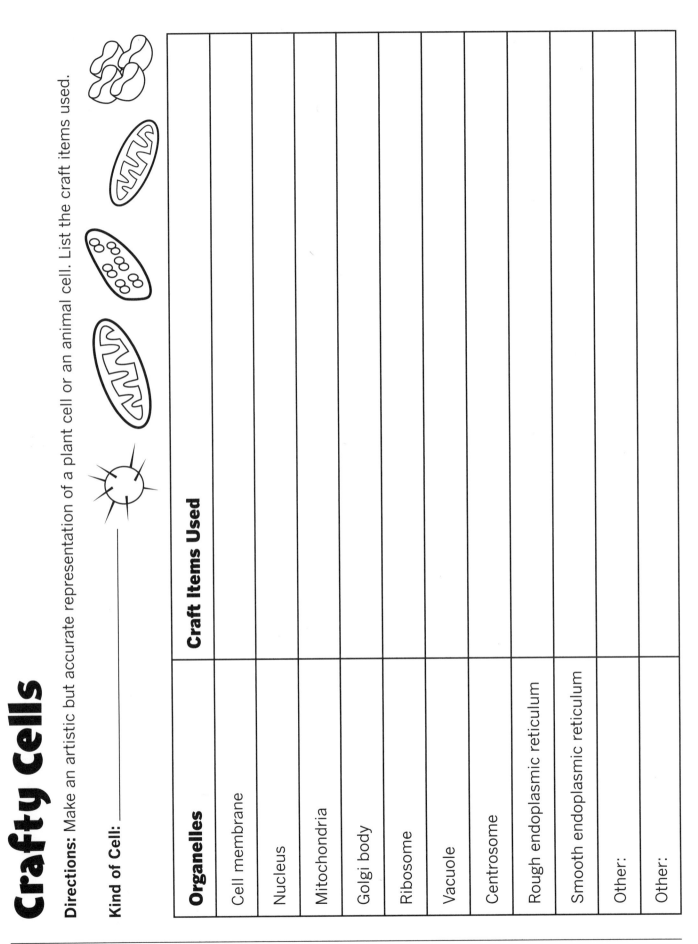

Organelles	**Craft Items Used**
Cell membrane	
Nucleus	
Mitochondria	
Golgi body	
Ribosome	
Vacuole	
Centrosome	
Rough endoplasmic reticulum	
Smooth endoplasmic reticulum	
Other:	
Other:	

978-1-4129-5925-4 • © Corwin Press

Most Like Me

Objectives

Students will explain the differences between phenotype and genotype. Students will identify and compare phenotypic traits.

> **Materials**
> - Most Like Me reproducible
> - overhead projector and transparency

Humans are 99.9% identical at the DNA level. It's the other 0.1% that makes each of us unique. Our genetic consistencies and variations (genotype) are passed down from generation to generation and displayed as physical traits (phenotype). Most human traits are multi-factorial, determined by a combination of genes (dominant and recessive genes) and environmental influences. In this game, students search for their closest phenotypic match among their classmates.

1. Write *phenotype* and *genotype* on the board and invite students to compare them. Explain that *phenotype* is an organism's observable physical traits, such as eye color or hair color, whereas *genotype* is the set of genes that determines each trait. A person's genotype, or genetic code, is the sum of all genes inherited from both parents, which are then expressed as the phenotype.

2. Give each student two or three copies of the **Most Like Me reproducible (page 43)** and display a copy on the overhead projector to guide instruction. Use the following definitions to explain the traits listed on the chart and pictured on the page:
   - **Tongue Rolling:** The ability to roll the tongue into a closed tube.
   - **Earlobe Attachment:** Earlobes are considered attached if they are connected directly to the side of the face.
   - **Mid-Digital Finger Hair:** If the middle segment of any finger has hair on it, even if it is only one hair, the person is considered to have this trait.
   - **Widow's Peak:** The forehead hairline dips like the top of a heart.
   - **Hitchhiker's Thumb:** A hitchhiker's thumb bends past vertical.
   - **Dimples:** Indentations in the cheeks, especially noticeable when smiling.
   - **Cleft Chin:** An indentation in the center of the chin.

3. Instruct the class to list each student's name on their Most Like Me chart, writing their own name first. Explain that the goal of the game is for students to find their closest phenotypic match among their classmates, using their chart to help them record and compare results.
4. Give students 20 minutes to complete their chart and evaluate their results. Encourage them to move around the room and survey their classmates.
5. Invite students to share their findings and name their closest phenotypic match.
6. Check their results by reading aloud each trait and having students raise their hand if they have that trait. (Encourage students to self-check their results during that time.) Challenge them to name the pair of students that is the most alike.

Extended Learning

- Invite a geneticist or genetic counselor to speak to the class about genetic disorders, such as Down's syndrome, cystic fibrosis, and sickle cell anemia. Encourage students to research and find out more about these conditions.
- Have students make a family tree to show one or more physical traits passed down from generation to generation. Use the following example as a guide.

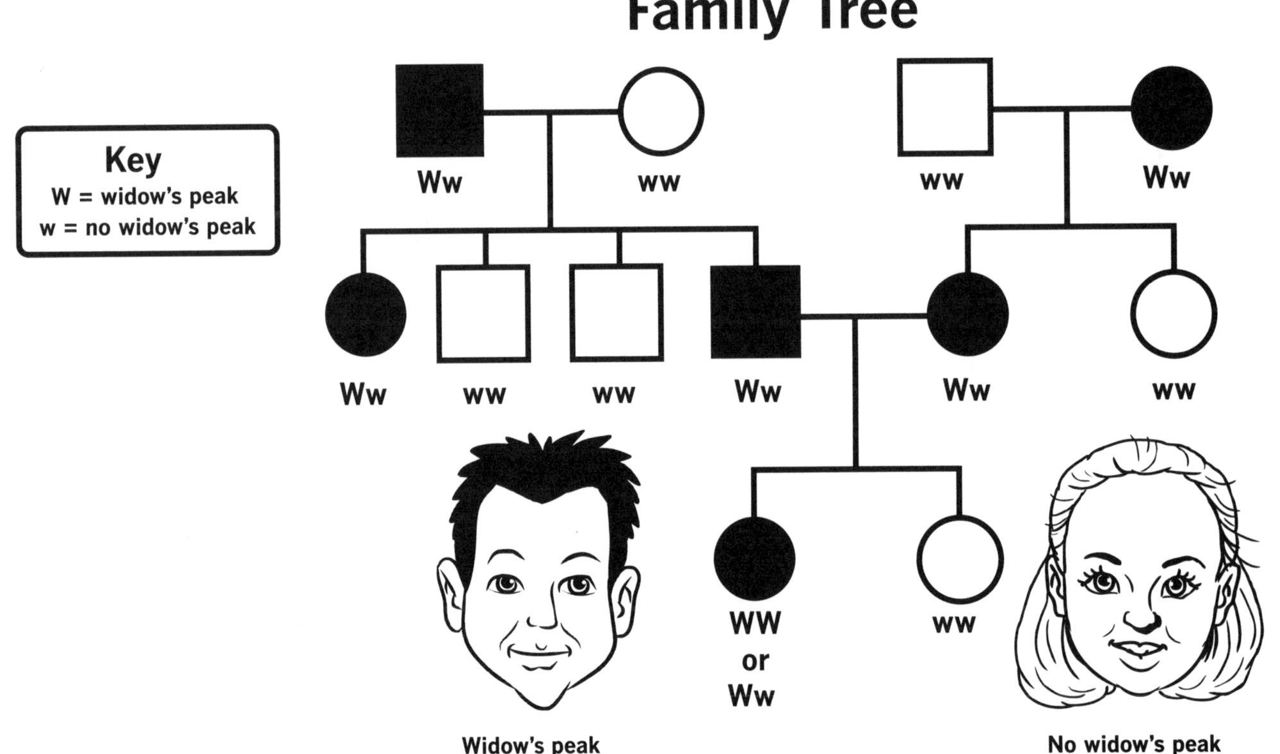

978-1-4129-5925-4

Name ______________________ Date ______________

Most Like Me

Directions: Find your closest phenotypic match before time is up! Fill out the first line about your own phenotype, writing *yes* or *no* for each trait. Then survey your classmates and record their traits. Who is the most like you?

Student's Name	Tongue Rolling?	Earlobes Attached?	Mid-Digital Finger Hair?	Widow's Peak?	Hitchhiker's Thumb?	Dimples in Both Cheeks?	Cleft Chin?

Animal Adaptations

Materials

- Animal Adaptations reproducible
- cardstock or index cards
- scissors
- glue
- reference materials about animals

Objective

Students will identify and describe different structural and behavioral adaptations of animals.

Animals rely on a variety of physical traits to help them survive in their environment, such as the shape of their body, the use of special features such as claws, or the color and thickness of their fur. These physical adaptations do not develop during a single lifetime but rather over many generations. In this game, students explore a variety of physical adaptations that help animals survive.

1. Use the **Animal Adaptations reproducible (page 46)** to make a set of game cards, showing the animal on the front of the card and listing its adaptive features on the back. For example:

   Camels: Camels have long eyelashes, thick eyebrows, and nostrils that can open and close to shield the face from sand and sunrays; a back hump of fat to enable them to go a long time without food or water; thick lips to eat prickly desert plants without pain; wide feet to walk on sand more easily; body temperature fluctuation for conservation of water and reduced sweating; and camouflage for the desert environment.

   Geckos: Geckos have special feet with flattened toes and scales for gripping and climbing easily; a tail that falls off and regenerates if grabbed; sharp teeth to penetrate the exoskeleton of insects; and camouflage among green and brown plants.

   Giraffes: Giraffes have a long neck to feed among treetops and to spot predators; an extra large heart to pump blood up the long neck; a long and tough prehensile tongue to pull leaves from branches; and a spotted coat for camouflage among trees.

   Hedgehogs: Hedgehogs are covered with thousands of sharp, needle-like spines that do not easily break. They are resistant to bee and wasp venom as well as to some poisonous frogs and snakes. They can roll into a tight ball and hiss when threatened; shudder and jerk their body when touched, driving spines into the skin of the predator; self-anoint when eating poisonous animals, chewing them until a froth forms and then licking the froth onto their own spines for further protection; and hibernate in cold weather or during times of little food or water.

978-1-4129-5925-4

Lions: Lions have a thick mane to make the male look bigger and protect the throat; loose belly skin to reduce injury if kicked; eyes in the front of the face for depth perception when stalking or ambushing prey; forepaws with long, retractile claws for grabbing and holding prey; a rough tongue to lick meat off bones; and a sandy body color for camouflage on the plains.

Polar Bears: Polar bears have fur made of hollow hairs that trap air and provide insulation; large furry feet that help to distribute their weight as they walk on ice; strong swimming skills and the ability to stay submerged for up to two minutes; and a white coat for camouflage in the Arctic environment. They hibernate during the coldest months.

2. Review with students the meaning of *adaptation*—a special trait that helps an organism survive in its environment. Ask students to name different types of structural and behavioral adaptations (e.g., shape, body feature, body temperature, hibernation, migration, camouflage, mimicry) and give examples of each type.

3. Then divide the class into two teams and explain that they will play a game about naming different animal adaptations. When you show an animal picture, teams take turns calling out adaptations that help the animal survive. The last team to say a correct trait wins the card. If they say a trait already mentioned, the other team wins the card. The team that collects the most cards wins the game.

4. After playing a class version of the game, divide the class into small groups and give them reference materials and supplies to make their own set of animal adaptation cards. Have them exchange cards with another group to play the game. Tell students to take turns being the game leader and show cards for classmates to win.

Extended Learning

- Have students create and play a plant adaptation version of the game.
- Ask students to make a picture book or field guide describing and illustrating animal adaptations.
- Invite students to choose one type of adaptation (such as camouflage, defense, or food gathering) and create a poster about it that provides facts and pictures.

Animal Adaptations

Nature A to Z

Objectives

Students will learn about the diversity of living things in our world. Students will identify and classify plants and animals by structure, function, and other common characteristics.

Materials

- Nature A to Z Game Board reproducible
- index cards
- 2 different colors of counters
- reference materials about plant and animal classification

Taxonomy is the classification or grouping of living and nonliving things by common attributes. By using a system of classification to categorize organisms, biologists are able to organize, study, and keep track of the millions of different living things in our world. In this game, students use their knowledge of classification to name plants and animals that belong to each selected category.

1. Introduce the game by discussing classification in general. Ask: *Why do we classify things around us? How do we classify them?* Explain that classification makes it easier to identify, describe, and compare things in our environment.
2. Give each pair of students a copy of the **Nature A to Z Game Board reproducible (page 49)**, at least 12 index cards, and two different colors of counters (15 per student). Have students use their index cards to make classification cards, writing on each card a different category for classifying living things. For example:

Classification Categories		
producer	reptile	consumer
bird	decomposer	mammal
vertebrate	fish	invertebrate
angiosperm	amphibian	gymnosperm

3. Have students play Nature A to Z after you model and explain the game, as follows:
   a. Players take turns choosing a card from the facedown deck and reading the category aloud to another player.
   b. That player must say the name of an organism that belongs to the selected category. If correct, he or she gets to put one colored counter on the first letter of the organism's name on his or her game board, such as *F* for the amphibian *frog*.
   c. Players may not cover a letter more than once.
   d. If players disagree about whether an answer is correct, they can look up the answer in a reference book.
   e. After players use the entire deck of cards, they reshuffle and use the cards again.

f. The player with the most covered letters on his or her game board wins the game.

4. After the game, have students use index cards and reference materials to make a new set of game cards and play again.

Extended Learning

- Have students play a habitat version of the game in which they name a plant or an animal found in a particular habitat or biome.
- Invite students to play an outdoor version of the game in which players are only allowed to name objects they see in their surrounding environment.
- Encourage students to include other science topics in the game, such as physical science (elements, noble gases, compounds, simple machines) and earth science (planets, stars, weather, Earth's eras).
- Have students make A to Z posters of organisms for assigned categories and include illustrations and fun facts about those organisms.

978-1-4129-5925-4

Name ______________________ Date ____________

Nature A to Z Game Board

Directions: To play the game, cover the first letter of the organism you correctly name for each classification card. The player with the most covered letters wins.

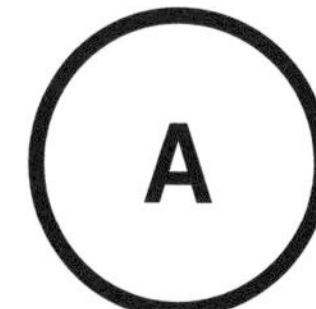

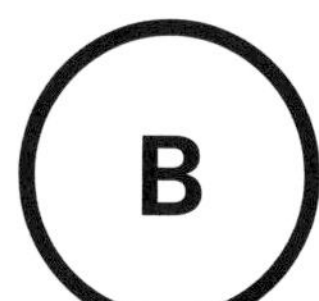

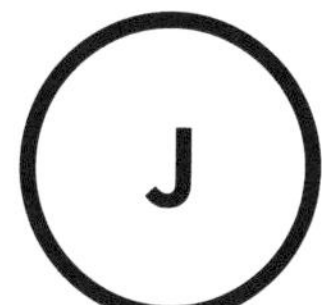

N

O

P

R

S

T

V

W

X

Y

Z

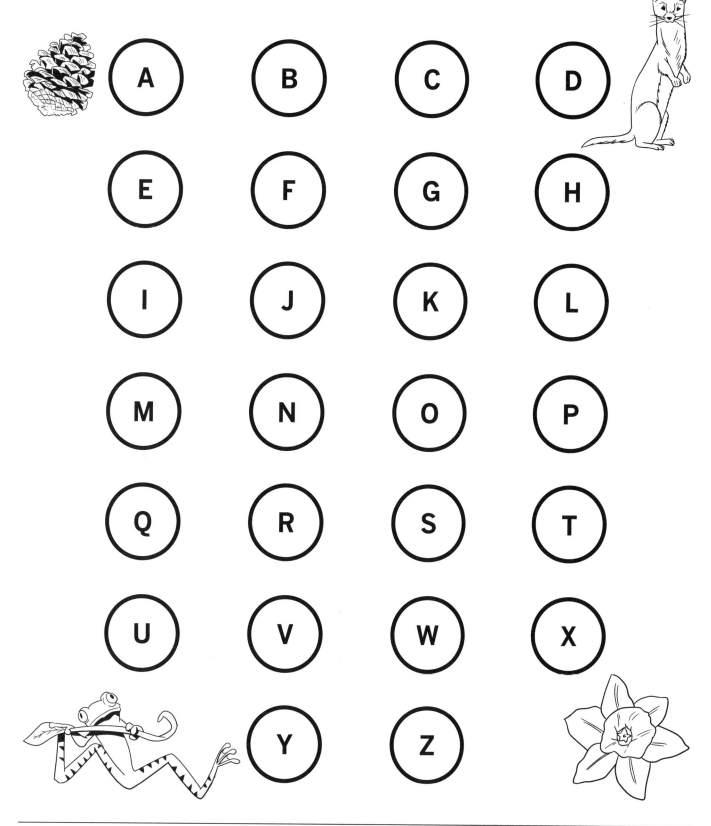

Who Am I?

Materials

- Who Am I? reproducible
- Physical Traits Key reproducible
- colored pencils or markers
- writing paper
- clipboards or hardbound books

Objectives

Students will distinguish between a person's phenotype and genotype. Students will draw and interpret symbolic phenotypic pictures of faces.

The phenotype of an individual includes eye color, hair color, and other observable traits. Each trait is determined by a set of genes, or genotype, inherited from both parents. In this game, students draw symbolic faces showing their own phenotype and then race to identify the portraits of their classmates.

1. Review with students the definitions of *phenotype* (physical traits) and *genotype* (the genetic code determining each trait). Invite students to brainstorm different types of phenotypic traits as you list their suggestions on the board.
2. Give students copies of the **Who Am I?** and **Physical Traits Key reproducibles (pages 52–53)**. Draw a sample face like the one shown and have students refer to the Physical Traits Key to identify each facial feature.
3. Tell students to use their reproducibles to secretly draw a symbolic face showing their own facial features. Tell them to write their name on the back of their paper.
4. Collect the drawings and label the front of each paper with a different letter of the alphabet. (Write double letters, such as *AA*, after you use all 26 letters.) Tape the drawings around the classroom to create a "gallery of faces."
5. Then give each student a sheet of writing paper and a clipboard (or hardbound book) to play the game *Who Am I?* Explain that they will have 20 minutes to match each face to the correct student, recording the matches on their paper (e.g., *A–Teresa; B–Jamal; C–Hector*). Give students time to set up their paper, listing the letter labels in alphabetical order down the left side of the page.
6. Begin the game, reminding students not to compare answers or talk to each other as they try to find the most matches. Encourage them to refer to their Physical Traits Key to help them identify each classmate's picture.
7. After 20 minutes, remove the pictures and have students return to their seats. Hold up each picture in front of the class, read aloud the label and name, and have students self-check their answers

978-1-4129-5925-4

(or have them exchange papers and check each other's work). The student with the most matches wins the game.

8. Follow-up the game by asking volunteers to share physical and behavioral traits they share with specific family members. Ask questions such as: *Who do you look most like in your family? Did you inherit any special talents or skills from a family member? Do you share certain interests with someone in your family?*

Extended Learning

- Have students select one of the traits from the Who Am I? game and draw a Punnett square to show the possible genotypes.
- Invite students to construct "DNA jewelry" by stringing different-colored beads on jewelry wire or fishing line to represent strands of DNA.

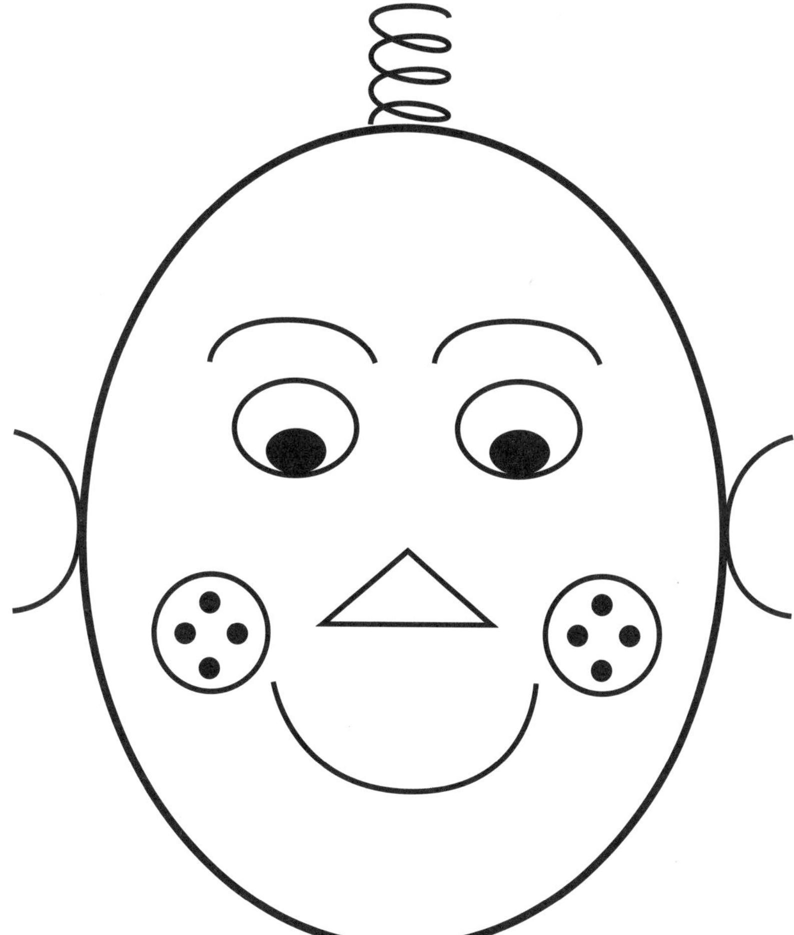

This face represents a female with curly hair, no widow's peak, blue eyes, wide nose, unattached earlobes, dimples and freckles, no cleft chin, and a tongue that rolls.

Name ______________________________ Date ______________

Who Am I?

Directions: Use the Physical Traits Key to draw your face showing specific facial features. Draw the correct symbols in the oval below to complete your portrait.

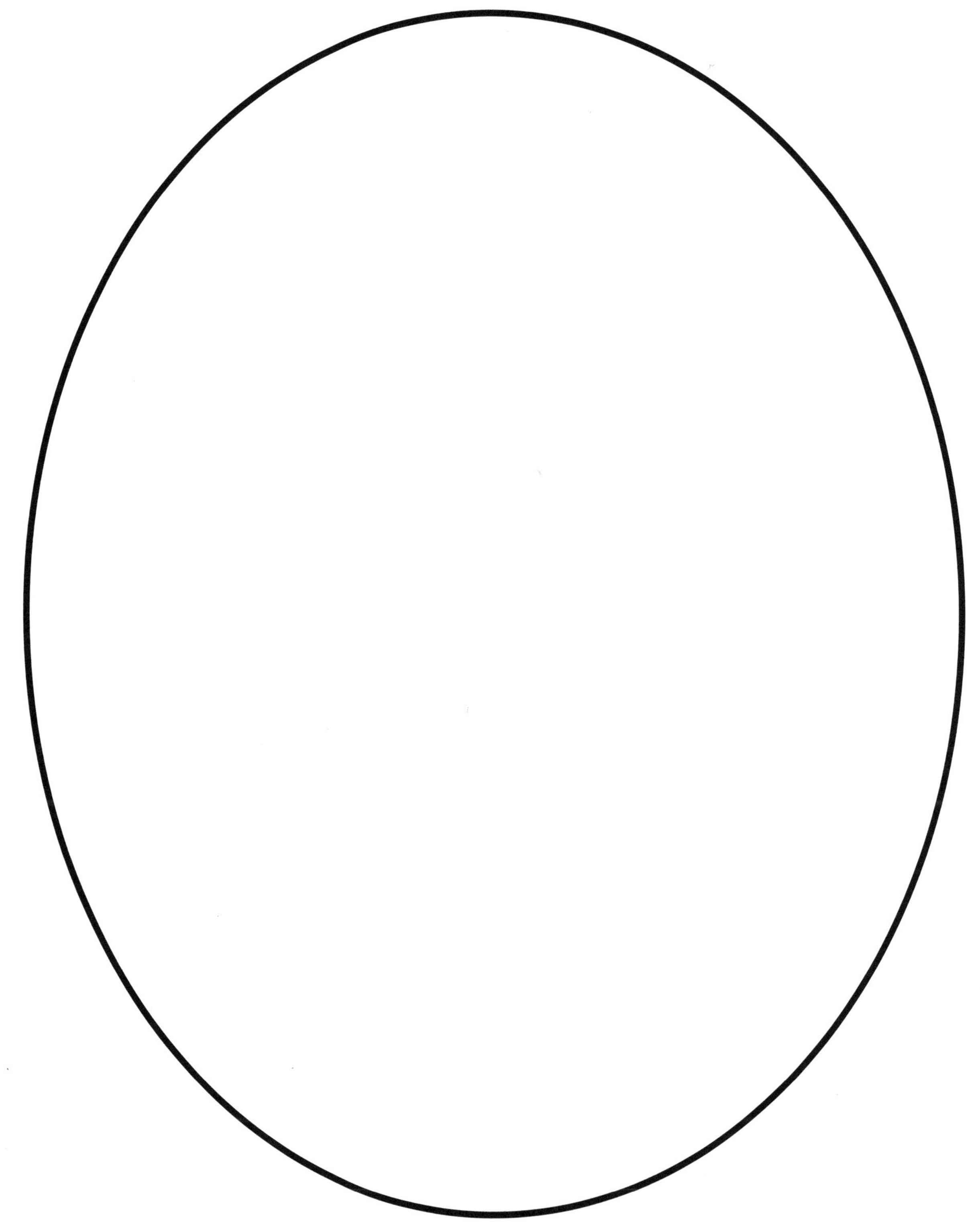

 Reproducible

Name ______________________________ Date ______________

Physical Traits Key

Directions: Use this key to complete the Who Am I? portrait for your own phenotype. Draw the correct symbol to represent each facial feature.

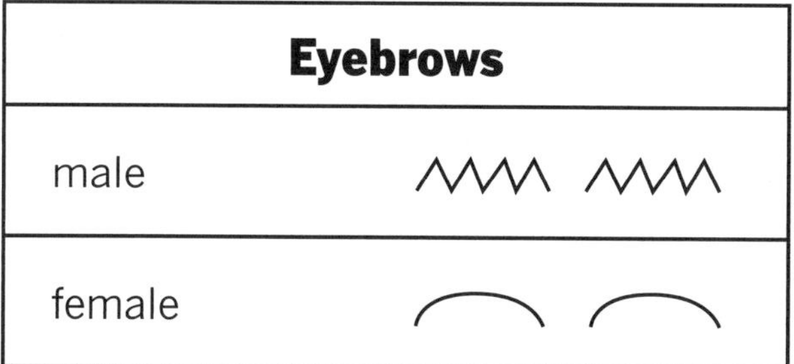

Eyebrows
male
female

Eye Color
green
brown
blue
hazel

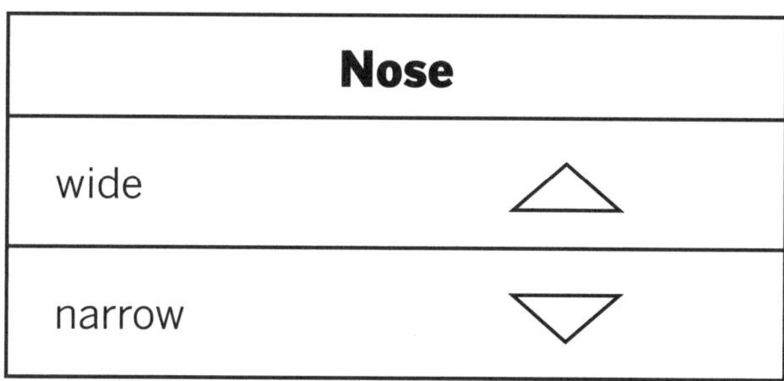

Nose
wide
narrow

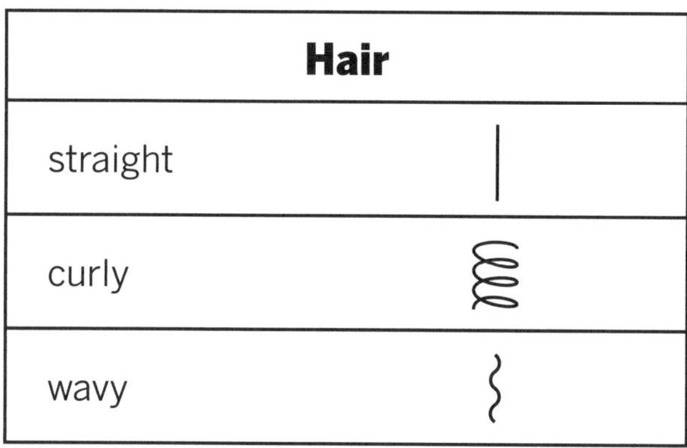

Hair
straight
curly
wavy

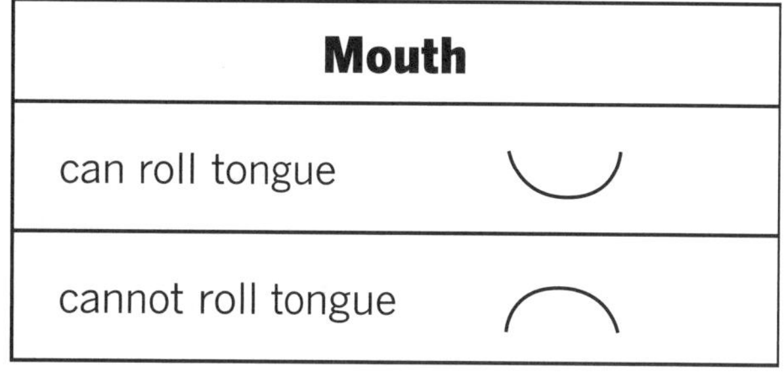

Mouth
can roll tongue
cannot roll tongue

Earlobes
attached
not attached

Cheeks
dimple
freckles

Forehead
widow's peak hairline

Chin
cleft in chin

Organ Picture Charades

Materials

- Organ Clue Cards reproducible
- cardstock
- scissors
- envelopes
- individual white boards or chart paper
- colored markers
- sand timers
- index cards

Objective

Students will identify and describe organs and organ systems.

The human body consists of several organ systems working simultaneously to keep the body functioning. Within each system are individual organs that perform specific jobs, such as the heart pumping blood, the lungs absorbing oxygen, and the stomach digesting food. In this activity, students play a game of Organ Picture Charades to review the features and functions of different organ systems.

1. For each group of four to six students, copy the **Organ Clue Cards reproducible (page 56)** onto cardstock and cut out the cards. Store each set of cards in a separate envelope.
2. Write *Organ Systems* on the board and invite students to share what they know about the 11 human organ systems (circulatory, digestive, respiratory, excretory, endocrine, immune, reproductive, muscular, nervous, skeletal, skin). Explain that they will take a closer look at these systems by playing a game of Organ Picture Charades.
3. Use the following set of clues to model how to play the game: *I am part of the circulatory system. I am a muscle with a beat. I pump blood. What part of the body do these clues describe?* Invite a volunteer to draw on the board something that would make the class guess the correct answer. *(heart)* Explain that players may only draw pictures; they may not speak or write words.
4. Divide the class into teams of two or three students and then pair up the teams to play the game. Give each group a set of the Organ Clue Cards, a white board or chart paper, colored markers, and a sand timer.
5. Explain the rules to students and then invite them to play Organ Picture Charades.
    a. The first player selects a clue card from the facedown stack and reads it silently without saying anything to his or her teammate(s).
    b. The player has one minute (or the duration of the sand timer) to draw any picture that will help his or her teammate(s) guess the correct organ described on the card. If the player accidentally says something, the other team gets the card.
    c. If a teammate correctly guesses the answer before time runs out, that team wins the card. If not, the team must give the card to a player on the other team so they can try to guess.

978-1-4129-5925-4

d. The game continues with teams taking turns selecting cards and drawing clues. The team with the most cards at the end of the game wins.

6. After students finish playing the game, suggest that they use index cards to make another set of clue cards to trade with another group, and then play the game again.

Extended Learning

- Have students trace each other on sheets of butcher paper and draw or paste pictures of organs inside the outlines to show the different organ systems. You might also have them include "flip-up facts," with questions written on the front of folded cards and the corresponding answers written inside.
- Invite students to make a human body picture book that includes illustrations and factual information about major organs and organ systems. They can each make their own book, or they can make one page of a collaborative class book.
- Invite a doctor or nurse to speak to the class about human anatomy and careers in medicine.

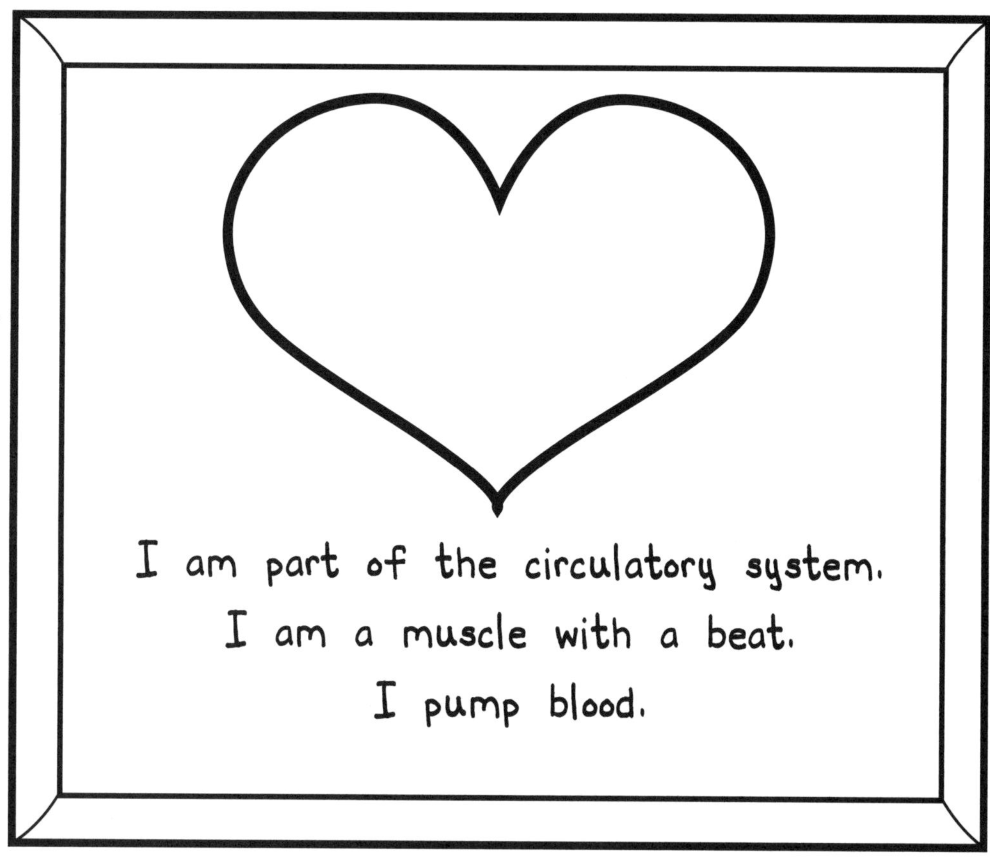
I am part of the circulatory system.
I am a muscle with a beat.
I pump blood.

Organ Clue Cards

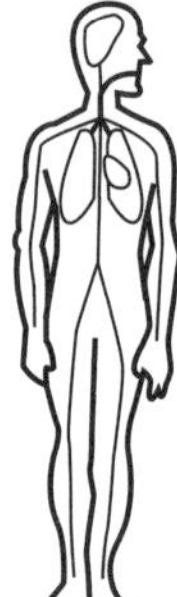

I am part of the central
nervous system.
I am made of
convoluted gray matter.
I think, therefore, I am.

I am part of the
digestive system.
I remove toxins
from the blood.
Cirrhosis hardens me.

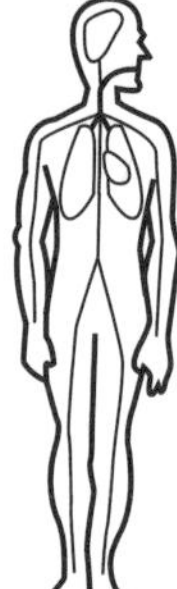

I am part of the
respiratory system.
I am protected by
the ribcage.
I have a twin.

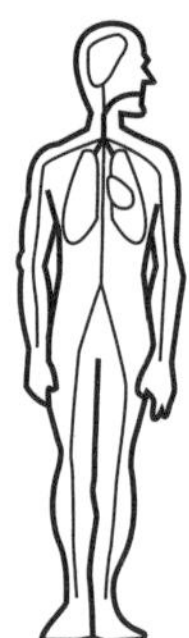

I am a part of the
nervous system.
I have a twin.
I can see you!

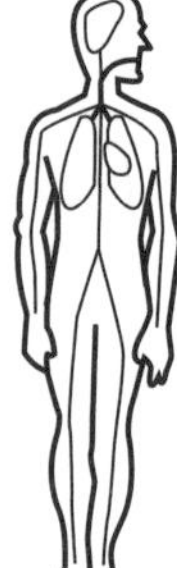

I am a bundle
of cells and fibers.
There are over 600 of
me in your body.
I help you move your bones.

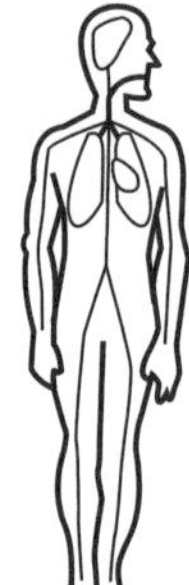

I am a
watertight container.
I can heal myself when
I'm hurt. I am flexible
so you can bend and stretch.

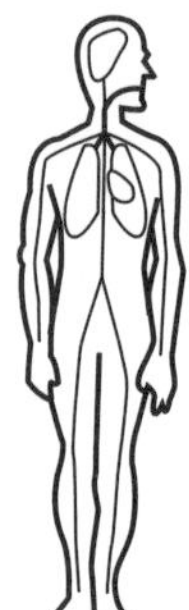

I am part of the
digestive system.
At almost five meters
long, I am the
longest section of
the digestive tract.
I am very twisty.

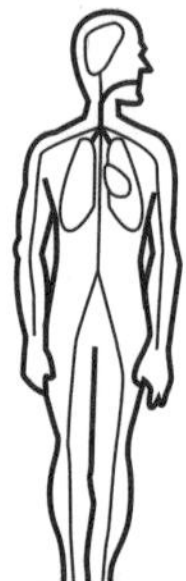

I am a hollow,
collapsible, muscular sac.
I can hold about
a pint of liquid.
I store urine produced
by the kidneys.

Genetics Guess-It!

Objective

Students will review genetics vocabulary.

A student's understanding of human genetics is highly dependent on knowing genetics terminology. In this game, students give descriptive clues about secret vocabulary words without using words that are off limits or taboo.

Materials

- Genetics Guess-It! Game Cards reproducible
- cardstock
- scissors
- envelopes
- index cards
- science textbooks, dictionaries, thesauruses

1. For each group of four to six students, copy the **Genetics Guess-It! Game Cards reproducible (page 59)** onto cardstock and cut out the cards. Store each set of cards in a separate envelope.
2. Write *Genetics* on the board and list the words *gene, DNA,* and *cellular* below it. Draw an *X* in front of each listed word. Explain to students that they will play a game called Genetics Guess-It! in which they say one-word clues to try to prompt their teammates to guess a specific vocabulary word. The challenge is to give clues without using the words listed on the game cards. These words are not allowed! Ask: *What one-word clues can we use to describe genetics without using any of these words marked with an* **X**, *or any part of those words?* (Possible answers: *chromosomes, nuclear, heredity, science, topic*)
3. Divide the class into teams of three or four students and then pair up the teams to play the game. Give each group a set of Genetics Guess-It! Game Cards and scrap paper for scorekeeping.
   a. To play the game, players take turns choosing a card from the facedown deck and giving one-word clues to their teammates about the target vocabulary word. They cannot use any words marked with an *X* (or any parts of those words).
   b. After each clue, teammates try to guess the correct answer. Teams may guess only one answer per clue (not multiple guesses from different teammates).
   c. For every clue given, the team gets one checkmark. After five checkmarks, players place the card at the bottom of the deck, and the next team gets a turn.
   d. If a player accidentally gives a forbidden word (or any part of that word) as a clue, the team automatically gets five checkmarks and loses their turn.
   e. After all the cards have been played, the team with the fewest checkmarks wins.

4. After students finish the game, have them use index cards and reference materials (textbooks, dictionaries, thesauruses) to make another set of game cards. Ask them to exchange cards with another group to play the game again.

Extended Learning

- Encourage students to make game cards that include vocabulary from different strands of science (life science, physical science, earth science, space science).
- Have students write and perform a humorous skit or play that incorporates vocabulary words used in the game.
- Ask students to design humorous posters that include jokes, riddles, and cartoons that will help them remember important vocabulary words.

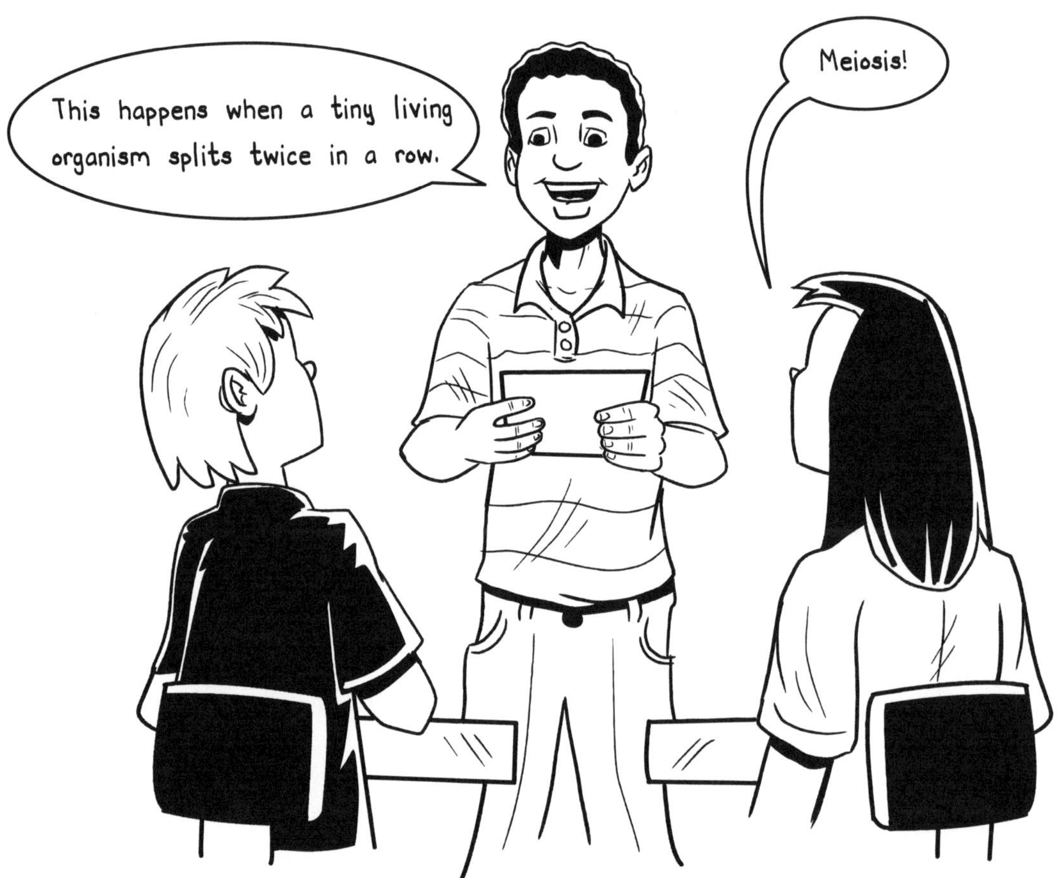

 978-1-4129-5925-4

Genetics Guess-It! Game Cards

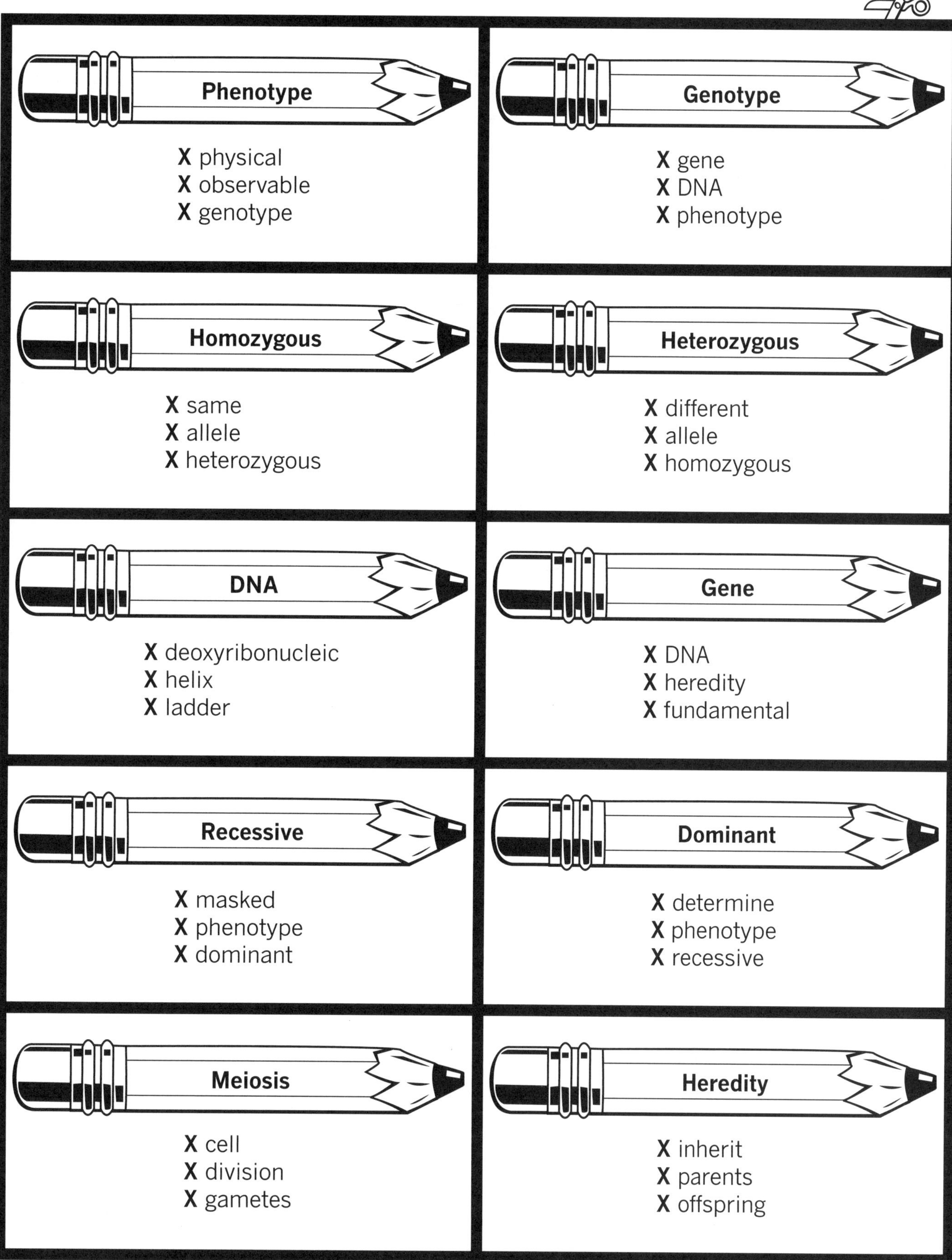

Phenotype
X physical
X observable
X genotype
Genotype
X gene
X DNA
X phenotype
Homozygous
X same
X allele
X heterozygous
Heterozygous
X different
X allele
X homozygous
DNA
X deoxyribonucleic
X helix
X ladder
Gene
X DNA
X heredity
X fundamental
Recessive
X masked
X phenotype
X dominant
Dominant
X determine
X phenotype
X recessive
Meiosis
X cell
X division
X gametes
Heredity
X inherit
X parents
X offspring

Homeostasis Millionaire

Materials
- Homeostasis Millionaire Game Cards reproducible
- reference materials about homeostasis and body regulation
- index cards

Objective
Students will explore different ways the body self-regulates in order to maintain homeostasis.

Homeostasis is the process of keeping a system in balance. The human body self-regulates in order to maintain constant internal conditions regardless of external conditions. In this game, students answer a series of challenging questions about homeostasis in an effort to win increasing amounts of money.

1. Ask students if they have ever seen the game show *Who Wants to Be a Millionaire®?* Invite them to share what they know about the game. Then tell them that they will be participating in a scientific game played similarly to Who Wants to Be a Millionaire?® (a registered trademark of Celador International Limited Corporation).
2. Use the sample cards from the **Homeostasis Millionaire Game Cards reproducible (page 62)** to explain and demonstrate how to play the game. Invite several volunteers to act as game show hosts, reading aloud the questions for other students to answer.
   a. Players answer multiple-choice questions at increasing levels of difficulty in order to win larger amounts of money, starting at $100 and moving up to $1,000,000. They must decide after each question whether to keep what they have already earned or to risk losing it by answering the next question for more money.
   b. Players have access to three "lifesavers," which allow them to get help from different sources. They may use each lifesaver only once. The three lifesavers are:
      - **50/50:** Two wrong answers are eliminated, leaving only two possible answers.
      - **Poll the Class:** Players read aloud each answer, and classmates silently indicate by a show of hands which answer they think is correct.
      - **Ask a Scientist:** Players choose one classmate to help answer the question.
   c. There are two "safe levels" of $2,000 and $64,000. If players reach those levels without making a mistake, they win at least that amount of money. If they answer a subsequent question incorrectly, they drop back down in earnings to that safe money amount. If players answer a question incorrectly before the $2,000 level, they win no money.

978-1-4129-5925-4

3. After the demonstration, divide the class into three teams and have each team make their own set of 15 game cards, writing questions of increasing difficulty. They should include four possible answers labeled *a*, *b*, *c*, and *d*, and circle the correct answer. Have them write the value of the question on the back of the card, writing increasing amounts accordingly: *$100; $200; $300; $500; $1,000; $2,000; $4,000; $8,000; $16,000; $32,000; $64,000; $125,000; $250,000; $500,000; $1,000,000.*

4. Collect the sets of game cards and use them to play three rounds of the game. Invite the students on one team to take turns answering the questions written by another team. Distribute the game cards to different members of the "audience" to read aloud in sequence. Have another volunteer record the team's progress on the board, writing the amount of money won and the lifesavers used.

5. Continue the game until the team answers a question incorrectly or reaches the million-dollar question. Then use another set of game cards to play a second round of the game with the next team. Repeat for the third team. The team with the greatest amount of money wins the competition.

Extended Learning

- Play different versions of the game by having students make game cards for other subject areas.
- Discuss the ways the immune system contributes to homeostasis. Then have groups of students write and perform a play in which the villain is an invading agent and the other characters are parts of the immune system.

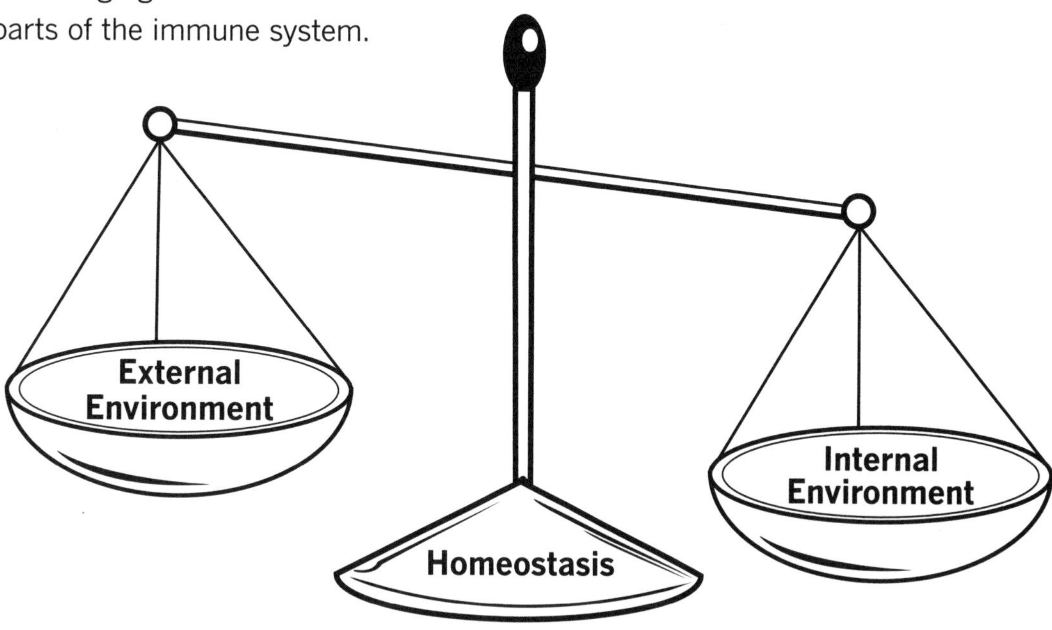

Homeostasis Millionaire Game Cards

The maintenance of an organism's internal environment is called:
a. compensating
b. homeostasis
c. balancing
d. routine

$100

The coordination of activities in an organism that maintain homeostasis in a constantly changing environment is called:
a. regulation
b. digestion
c. synthesis
d. respiration

$200

Our bodies try to maintain a constant temperature of about:
a. 100 °F
b. 98.6 °F
c. 75 °F
d. 20 °F

$300

If the environment gets cold, we will often shiver in order to:
a. keep body temperature the same as the external temperature
b. decrease body temperature
c. increase body temperature
d. regulate blood pressure

$500

Homeostasis in the human body is often maintained by a:
a. neutral feedback loop
b. solar feedback loop
c. positive feedback loop
d. negative feedback loop

$1,000

978-1-4129-5925-4 • © Corwin Press

Human Body Quiz Show

Objective

Students will write and answer questions about human biology and healthy habits, including body structure, organ systems, cellular structure, diseases, and nutrition.

For this variation of the popular game show *Jeopardy®* (a registered trademark of Jeopardy Productions, Inc. dba Merv Griffin Enterprises Corporation), students review human biology by answering trivia questions that classmates research and write on their own. They also compete in a whole-class version of the game. Students may play this game several times using other categories of science or other subject areas.

Materials

- Human Body Quiz Show reproducible
- overhead projector and transparency
- reference materials about the human body
- large sticky notes or index cards and tape

1. Invite students to share what they know about the game show *Jeopardy®*. Explain that each Jeopardy® clue shows an answer to a question, and players must say the correct question for that answer. For example, if the clue is: *This field of science is the study of living organisms,* the correct answer is: *What is biology?*
2. Display a transparency of the **Human Body Quiz Show reproducible (page 65)** to play a class version of the game. Divide the class into three teams and have teams take turns selecting a clue from the game board and answering it in the form of a question. For example, if a team asks for *Organ Systems for $100*, and the clue is: *A sac-like structure that stores urine,* the team should answer: *What is the bladder?* If the team answers correctly (see Answer Key on page 95), they earn that amount of money and take another turn. If they answer incorrectly, it's the next team's turn. The team with the most money at the end of the game wins.
3. Have small groups of students use sticky notes (or index cards and tape) to make different wall versions of the game. Tell them to write five clue cards for each of these six categories: *Body Structure, Organ Systems, Cells and Genetics, Diseases and Defenses, Health and Nutrition, Mystery Science* (any science). Remind students to include clues with increasing levels of difficulty valued at increasing amounts of money and to write the correct answers on the back of the cards. Have them tape the cards in columns on the wall to create the game board.
4. Have students use another group's setup to play the game in one of two ways:

   Version 1: One student is the host, reading aloud the selected clue cards. The other students are the players, working individually or in pairs to answer the clues correctly. If they answer correctly, they win that card (taking it from the wall) and get another turn. If they answer incorrectly, the game continues with the next player. The player with the greatest amount of money wins the game.

Version 2: Instead of a host, all students take turns reading aloud the clues chosen by each player. If players respond correctly, they win that card. If they respond incorrectly, they must remove the card from the game altogether (without anyone else getting a chance to win it). The game continues with the next player. The player with the greatest amount of money wins the game.

5. Invite groups to rotate to different games and play again.
6. Follow-up with a discussion by asking students for ways they could improve the game. List their suggestions on the board and come to a class consensus for creating a new game.

Extended Learning

- Have students use other science topics or subject matter for the game cards.
- Invite partners or small groups to create and present an instructional Web page or PowerPoint® presentation about one or more aspects of the human body.

Body Structure	Organ Systems	Cells and Genetics	Diseases and Defenses	Health and Nutrition	Mystery Science
$100	$100	$100	$100	$100	$100
$200	$200	$200	$200	$200	$200
$300	$300	$300	$300	$300	$300
$400	$400	$400	$400	$400	$400
$500	$500	$500	$500	$500	$500

978-1-4129-5925-4

Human Body Quiz Show

Body Structure	Organ Systems	Cells and Genetics	Diseases and Defenses	Health and Nutrition
$100 The frame holding up the body	**$100** A sac-like structure that stores urine	**$100** Another name for a fertilized egg	**$100** Any kind of disease that can pass from one organism to another	**$100** The simple or complex nutrients that are a major source of energy
$200 Another name for *thighbone*	**$200** The number of chambers in the heart	**$200** A group of similar cells that perform the same function	**$200** The type of cells that fight infection	**$200** Vitamin found in carrots that helps with eyesight
$300 The name and number of small bones in the backbone	**$300** Organs that filter blood and excrete toxins in the form of urine	**$300** Where genes are found in the nucleus of a cell	**$300** A disease caused by the body not producing enough insulin	**$300** Category with the fewest servings in the Food Guide Pyramid
$400 The two types of soft tissue inside bones	**$400** A flap that closes the trachea	**$400** The name given to different versions of the same gene	**$400** The role of B lymphocytes in an immune response	**$400** The measure of energy in food
$500 The four types of movable joints	**$500** This is formed by the division of the trachea	**$500** The four nucleotides of DNA	**$500** The four major groups of human pathogens	**$500** Any four of the six types of nutrients

CHAPTER 3

Earth and Space Science

What Am I?

Materials
- reference materials about natural resources
- index cards
- colored pencils and markers
- masking tape

Objective

Students will identify and investigate some of Earth's natural resources.

Humans use many of the earth's natural resources. Some of these resources can be reproduced relatively quickly and are considered renewable. Others, such as petroleum, are not easily reproduced and are nonrenewable. In this game, students will learn that natural resources are needed to produce common, everyday objects.

1. Write the column headers *Trees, Petroleum,* and *Minerals/ Metals* on the board. Ask students: *What do these things have in common?* Explain that they are all natural resources. Invite students to brainstorm products made from each resource as you list their correct suggestions on the board. For example:

Trees	Petroleum	Minerals/Metals
newspaper	gasoline	table salt
maple syrup	crayons	aluminum foil
corkboard	balloons	toothpaste

2. Provide students with reference materials (books, magazines, Internet access) and have them each make a game card showing one item made from a natural resource (other than those items listed). Ask them to include the name of the item, the name of the natural resource, and a picture of the item. Make sure students get your approval before they begin. Ensure that each student chooses a different item.

3. Collect the cards and redistribute them, telling students to keep them "secret." Explain that they will play a game in which they must correctly guess the "mystery item" taped to their back. Line up students, give them each a strip of tape, and have them tape their card to the back of the person in front of them.

4. Give students five minutes to try to figure out their mystery item. They may only ask each classmate one "yes" or "no" question about their item, and classmates may only answer *yes* or *no*. They may not ask for confirmation of a specific guess. For example, they may not ask: *Is the answer **gasoline**?* But they may ask: *Does it provide power for cars and trucks?*
5. After five minutes, ask students to return to their seats and take turns saying aloud the name of the item they think is written on their back. Have them pull off their card to see if they are correct.
6. Conclude the game by having students find all of their classmates with items made from the same resource. Have each group list their items on the board and brainstorm more items to add to the list.

Extended Learning

- Conduct class debates about the pros and cons of using specific natural resources. Invite audience members to ask questions and vote for a winner.
- Have each group work together to make a poster or a PowerPoint® presentation about their natural resource. Have them include pictures and factual information about different items made from that resource.
- Invite students to write a creative story or cartoon strip about an animal living in or near a natural resource area, such as a rainforest or a mining tunnel, and the effects caused by human "harvesting" or usage of those natural resources.

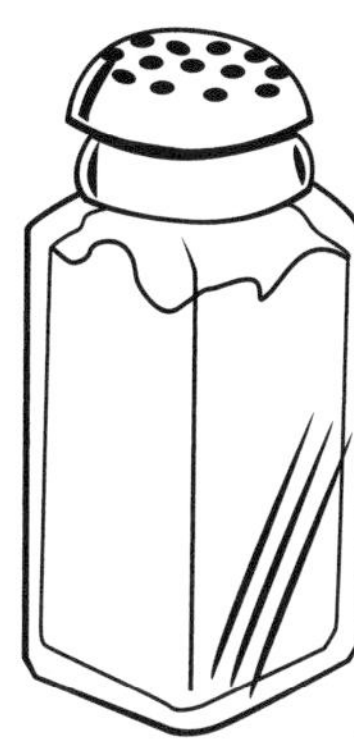

The Plate Game

Materials

- The Plate Game reproducible
- chart paper
- poster board
- art supplies
- index cards
- dice
- counters or other game pieces
- reference materials about plate tectonics, earthquakes, and volcanoes

Objectives

Students will research plate tectonics and its effect on the earth's crust. Students will learn how earthquakes, volcanoes, and mid-ocean ridges are formed.

The *plate tectonics* theory states that the earth's crust is broken into several pieces or *plates*, including the seven continents. These plates shift constantly on top of a mobile molten layer. Sometimes when two plates try to move past each other, they stick and then slip, causing an earthquake. In this game, students learn about plate tectonics and the types of landforms and events caused by the moving plates.

1. As a warm-up, help students complete a KWL chart about plate tectonics. Ask students to share what they *know* (K) and what they *want to know* (W) about the topic as you list their ideas on the chart. Tell students that they will complete the last column, what they *learned* (L), after playing a game.
2. Review the plate tectonics theory with students, in which the earth's outer surface, or lithosphere, is described as separate and distinct tectonic plates that move or shift. The plates meet at one of three types of boundaries:

   Divergent Boundaries: The plates spread apart from each other, forming a trench that is filled with new crustal material, often formed from molten magma below it. The Mid-Atlantic Ridge is a divergent boundary.

   Convergent Boundaries: The plates collide, forming either a continental collision (if they consist of continental crust) or a subduction zone (if one plate moves below the other). The Himalayas are the result of a convergent boundary.

   Transform Boundaries: The plates slide past each other along transform faults. The San Andreas Fault is a transform fault.

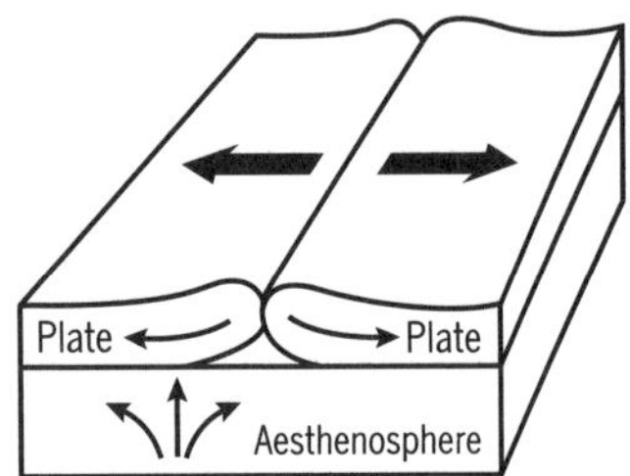

Divergent Boundary

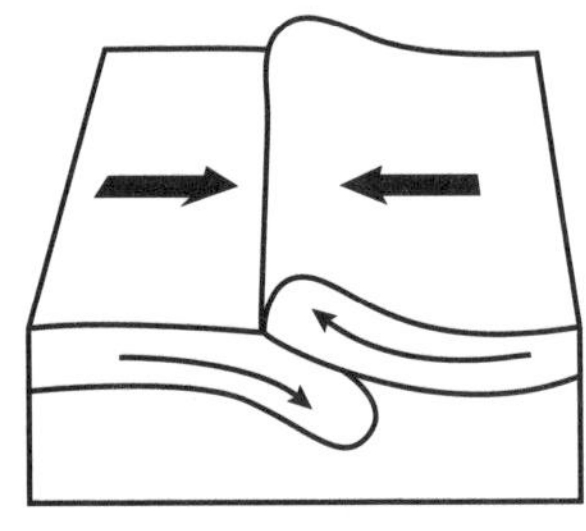
Convergent Boundary

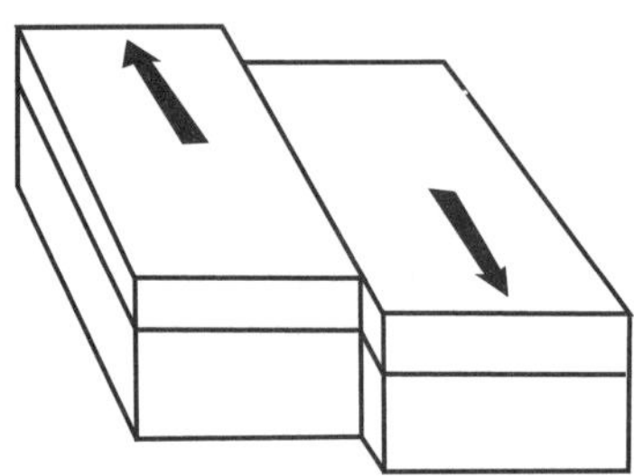
Transform Boundary

3. Give each group of three to five students a copy of **The Plate Game reproducible (page 70)** and the supplies needed to make the game (or have them gather and use their own supplies). Read the directions together and check for understanding. They can make their game in class or for homework. Encourage students to use reference materials and the KWL chart to help them write the questions for their cards. Tell them to write the questions on the front of the cards and the answers on the back.
4. Invite groups to present and explain their games in front of the class. Then give them time to play their games. After students play their own game, suggest that they trade games with another group and play each other's games.
5. Conclude the activity by having students complete the KWL chart. Invite volunteers to share what they learned from playing the games while you list their ideas on the chart.

Extended Learning

- Have students research and draw a map of the most dangerous volcanoes in the United States or the world. You might also have them make a working model of a volcano.
- Invite students to create a newspaper or television news report about a historic earthquake or volcanic eruption. Have them include details about what happened, where it happened, when it happened, how it affected lives, and the likelihood of it happening again. Allow time for students to share their reports.

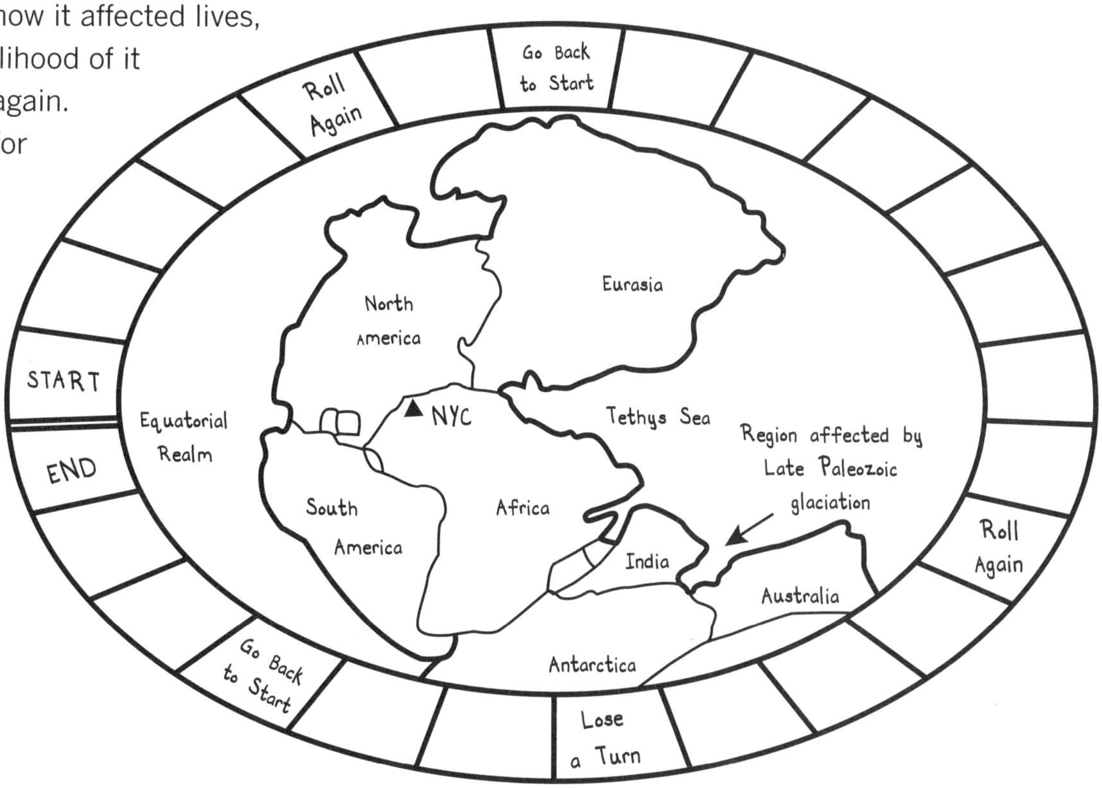

Name ________________________________ Date ______________

The Plate Game

Directions: Use poster board, index cards, game pieces, one die, and art supplies to make a game about Earth's crust, as described below.

Game Board

Make a game board that consists of at least 25 spaces. Include:

- One *Start* space and one *End* space
- At least one *Go Back to Start* space
- At least one *Roll Again* space
- At least one *Lose a Turn* space

Game Cards

Make a set of 24 game cards, each with a question on one side and the answer on the other side. Include:

- Six questions about the continental drift theory
- Six questions about plate tectonics, including plate movement
- Six questions about landforms created by plate tectonics
- Six questions about earthquakes and volcanoes

How to Play the Game

1. All players put their game piece on *Start.*
2. Place the game cards in a stack, facedown.
3. One player selects a game card and reads the question aloud to another player.
4. If the player answers correctly, he or she rolls the die and moves ahead that number of spaces. If the player answers incorrectly, he or she does not get to roll the die.
5. The next player takes a turn, choosing a game card to read aloud to another player.
6. The game continues, with players taking turns answering questions and moving their game pieces. The first player to reach the *End* space on an exact roll wins the game!

 Reproducible

Time Travel Crossword

Objectives

Students will learn about Earth's eras and the geologic time scale. Students will learn about primitive and prehistoric organisms that inhabited Earth.

The planet Earth has changed tremendously in its 4.6-billion-year existence. In this game, students review different time periods in Earth's history and how life has evolved over time. Players must use both their knowledge of earth science and their spelling skills to win the game.

Materials

- Time Travel Game Board reproducible
- Time Travel Game Cards reproducible
- reference materials about Earth's history
- cardstock
- colored pencils or pens
- scissors
- index cards

1. Review Earth's geologic time scale with students. Point out that during the last 4.6 billion years, many different life forms have existed. Ask questions such as: *How old is Earth?* (about 4.6 billion years) *How long ago did dinosaurs exist?* (about 250 million to 65 million years ago) *When did humans first appear on Earth?* (about 2 million years ago)
2. Ahead of time, photocopy the **Time Travel Game Cards reproducible (page 74)** on cardstock and cut out the cards for each student pair. For the game, give each pair a set of cards, a copy of the **Time Travel Game Board reproducible (page 73)**, and two different-colored pencils or pens (one per player). Have them put the cards facedown in a stack. Explain that the goal of the game is to correctly spell the answers to those questions on the game board and fill in the most spaces to win the game.
    a. Players take turns choosing game cards and reading the question aloud for the other player to answer.
    b. If the other player correctly states and spells the answer, he or she writes the answer horizontally or vertically on the game board, one letter per square.
    c. After the first player writes an answer, all other answers must include a letter from a previously written word on the game board, forming crosswords from top to bottom.
    d. If players answer incorrectly, the card goes back to the bottom of the stack.
    e. The player with the most filled spaces at the end of the game wins.

								T.
P	T	E	R	O	S	A	U	R
A								E
N								X
G	O	N	D	W	A	N	A	
A								
E								
A								

978-1-4129-5925-4

3. When students have played the game with the cards provided, have them use reference materials and index cards to make more game cards and continue the game or play again.

Extended Learning

- Have students make an Earth History Timeline that includes factual information and pictures of organisms living during the different time periods.
- Prompt students to make a dinosaur picture book that includes information about what dinosaurs ate, where they lived, and pictures of the dinosaurs. Suggest that one chapter of the picture book contain herbivores, one chapter carnivores, and one chapter omnivores. Have them also include a chapter about different extinction theories.
- Invite a paleontologist to speak to the class. Encourage students to take notes during the presentation and write a summary about what they learned.

978-1-4129-5925-4

Name ______________________________ Date ______________

Time Travel Game Board

Directions: With a partner, take turns writing answers to the Time Travel Game Cards, vertically or horizontally, one letter per square. (Each player uses a different-colored pen or pencil.) After your first turn, you must use a letter from a previously written answer. The player with the most squares filled wins.

Time Travel Game Cards

Question: Name the supercontinent formed from all of Earth's landmasses in the mid-Triassic period.

Answer: *Pangaea*

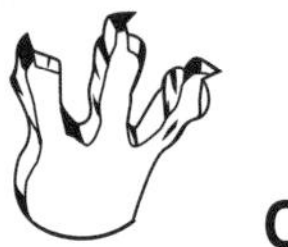

Question: When Pangaea broke up, it created two landmasses, one called Laurasia. Name the other landmass.

Answer: *Gondwana*

Question: Its name means "winged lizard" in Greek. It was as big as an airplane and could fly like one, too. Name this prehistoric reptile.

Answer: *pterosaur*

Question: It is sometimes called the "Age of Dinosaurs." Name this middle period of the Mesozoic Era, about 208 to 146 million years ago.

Answer: *Jurassic*

Question: This dinosaur was the largest land animal of all time. It had very long neck, and its name means "lizard footed." Name this dinosaur.

Answer: *sauropod*

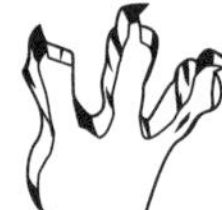

Question: The first microscopic, single-celled life forms appeared. In what era did this happen?

Answer: *Precambrian*

Question: This "tyrant lizard king" was a huge, meat-eating dinosaur that lived about 85 to 65 million years ago during the Cretaceous period. Name this dinosaur.

Answer: *Tyrannosaurus rex*

Question: These extinct, hard-shelled marine animals evolved during the Paleozoic era. They disappeared in the mass extinction at the end of the Permian period. Name this animal.

Answer: *trilobite*

Space Secrets

Objectives

Students will identify and describe celestial objects in our solar system. Students will describe equipment used in space exploration.

Materials

- Space Secrets Game Cards reproducible
- cardstock
- scissors
- envelopes
- timers
- index cards
- reference materials about the solar system and space exploration

Our solar system consists of a sun, eight planets, at least three dwarf planets, and many other celestial bodies orbiting those planets, including satellites, comets, and asteroids. In this game, students identify and describe different objects in our solar system and the equipment used to study and explore those objects.

1. Ahead of time, photocopy the **Space Secrets Game Cards reproducible (page 77)** on cardstock. Cut out a set of game cards for each group of six or eight students. Store each set in an envelope.
2. As a warm-up for the game, say the following words aloud, one word at a time, and invite students to guess what you're describing: *planet, third, ours.* (Earth)
3. Explain to students that they will play a game called Space Secrets, in which they say one-word clues about a celestial object or a piece of space equipment for teammates to guess using the fewest possible clues. The clues may not include any part of the description on the game card (or the answer). For example:

   Game Card Description: This planet is closest to the sun.

   Clues Not Allowed: planet, closest, sun, Mercury (or any part of those words)

   Possible Clue Words: first, smallest, globe, orbit, space, metallic

   Correct Answer: Mercury

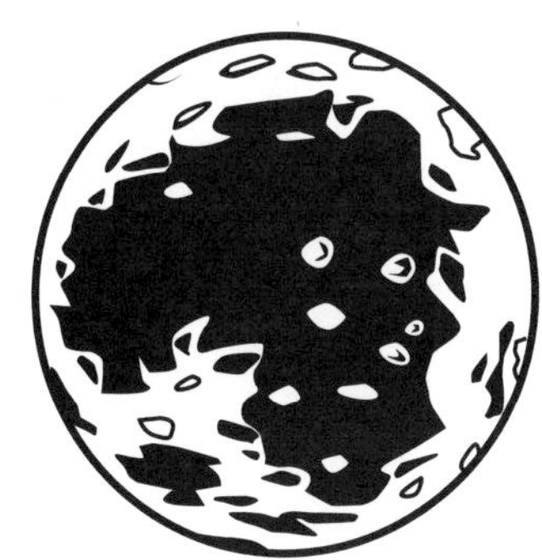

first, smallest, globe, orbit, space, metallic

4. Divide the class into teams of three or four students and then pair up the teams to play the game. Give each group a set of game cards and a timer. Have students place the cards facedown in a stack. Then model and explain the rules of the game:
   a. To begin the game, one player selects a game card, reads it silently, and tries to think of good clues for teammates.
   b. After the timer starts, the player begins to give one-word clues to teammates, trying to get them to guess the correct answer within one minute. The team may only guess one answer per clue.
   c. The other team keeps score, recording the number of clue words spoken before the correct answer is given. They also confirm the correct answer.

d. If the team does not guess the answer within one minute, the player places the card back at the bottom of the stack, and the other team takes a turn. Similarly, if a player uses a "forbidden" clue, play passes to the other team.

e. Teams continue to take turns, rotating the players giving clues, until all of the game cards have been used. The team with the *least* number of points wins.

5. When students finish playing the game with the cards provided, have them use index cards and reference materials to make another set of game cards. Then have them exchange cards with another group to play the game again.

Extended Learning

- Invite students to make a model of the solar system using art supplies or computer technology.
- Arrange a field trip to a nearby planetarium or observatory and have students write a summary about what they learned. You might also create a "Space Scavenger Hunt" for them to complete during the trip.
- Encourage students to write and share rhymes, songs, and different mnemonic devices to help them remember the order of the planets and other celestial facts.

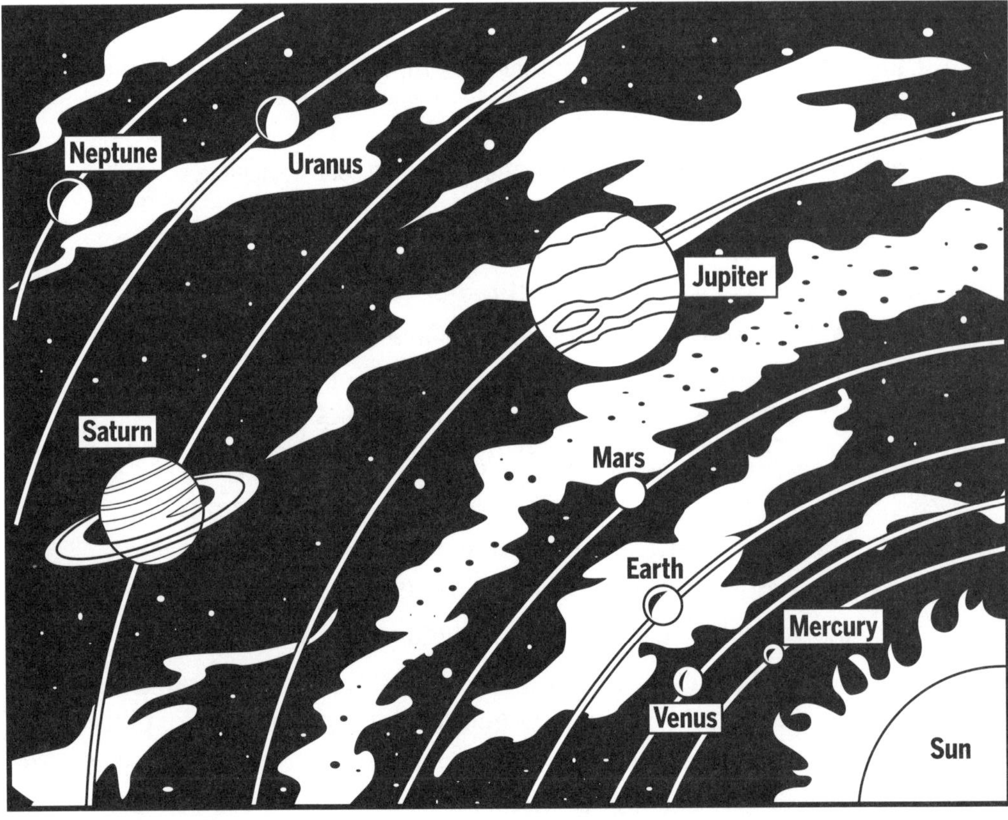

Space Secrets Game Cards

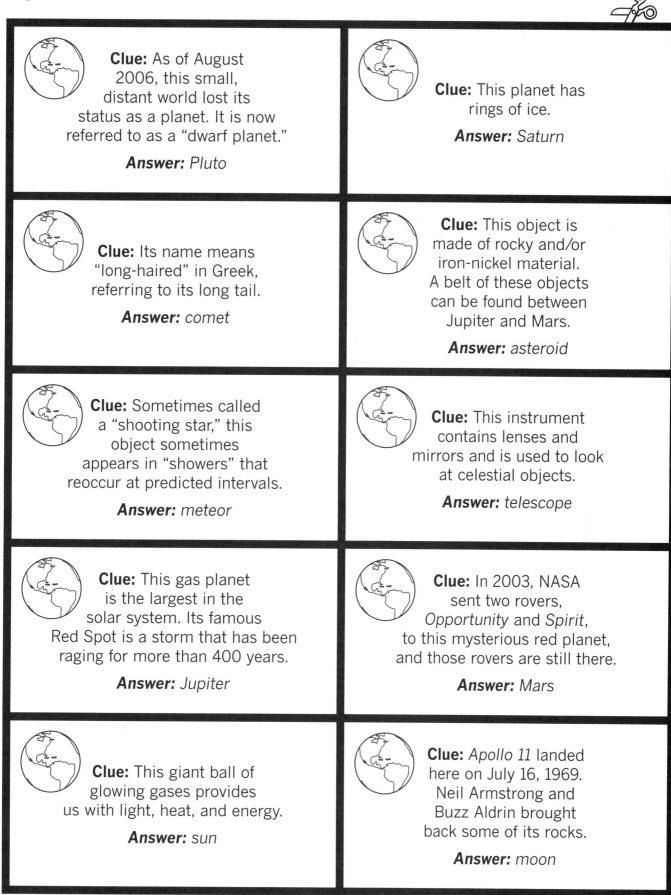

Clue: As of August 2006, this small, distant world lost its status as a planet. It is now referred to as a "dwarf planet."

Answer: *Pluto*

Clue: This planet has rings of ice.

Answer: *Saturn*

Clue: Its name means "long-haired" in Greek, referring to its long tail.

Answer: *comet*

Clue: This object is made of rocky and/or iron-nickel material. A belt of these objects can be found between Jupiter and Mars.

Answer: *asteroid*

Clue: Sometimes called a "shooting star," this object sometimes appears in "showers" that reoccur at predicted intervals.

Answer: *meteor*

Clue: This instrument contains lenses and mirrors and is used to look at celestial objects.

Answer: *telescope*

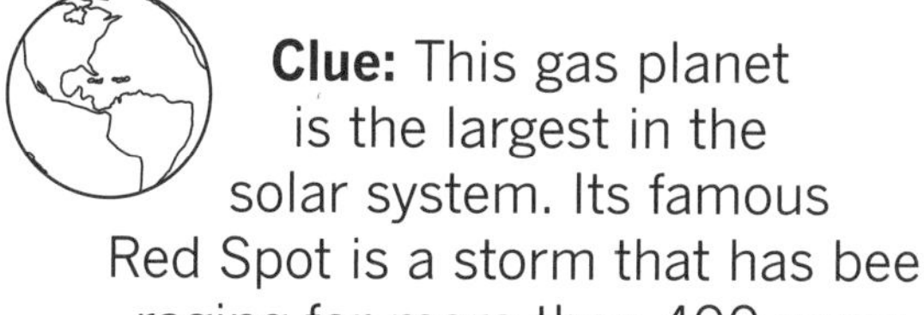

Clue: This gas planet is the largest in the solar system. Its famous Red Spot is a storm that has been raging for more than 400 years.

Answer: *Jupiter*

Clue: In 2003, NASA sent two rovers, *Opportunity* and *Spirit*, to this mysterious red planet, and those rovers are still there.

Answer: *Mars*

Clue: This giant ball of glowing gases provides us with light, heat, and energy.

Answer: *sun*

Clue: *Apollo 11* landed here on July 16, 1969. Neil Armstrong and Buzz Aldrin brought back some of its rocks.

Answer: *moon*

Earth Cycles Pyramid

Materials

- Earth Cycles Pyramid Game Cards reproducible
- cardstock
- scissors
- tape
- envelopes
- timers
- index cards
- reference materials about Earth's cycles

Objective

Students will research and describe different Earth cycles, including water, atmospheric, rock, nitrogen, and carbon cycles.

Earth is a dynamic system of cycles, all working together in equilibrium. A change in one cycle can cause changes in others. In this game, students use their knowledge of these cycles to answer a pyramid of questions before time runs out.

1. For each group of four students, copy the **Earth Cycles Pyramid Game Cards reproducible (page 80)** onto cardstock. Cut out the cards and fold along the dotted line. Tape the edges together to make a set of double-sided game cards (value and topic on one side, list of words on the other). Store each set of cards in an envelope.
2. Review the water cycle with students. Write *rain* on the board and ask: *Where does rain come from?* (clouds) *What happens when rain hits land?* (It soaks into the ground or goes into oceans, rivers, or streams.) *How does water get back into the clouds?* (evaporation) Invite volunteers to help draw the water cycle on the board. Explain that the water cycle is just one of several cycles on Earth. Invite students to list others. *(atmospheric, rock, nitrogen, carbon, plate tectonics)*
3. Give each group of four students a set of Earth Cycles Pyramid Game Cards and a timer. Have each group divide into pairs to form teams. Then model and explain how to play the game:
   a. Arrange the game cards in a pyramid of three rows: one $150 question on top, two $100 questions in the middle, and three $50 questions on the bottom.

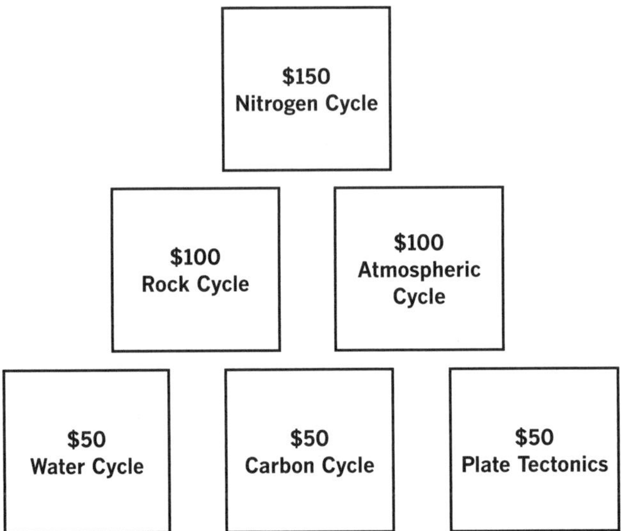

978-1-4129-5925-4

b. A player on the first team calls out a topic and money value, such as: *Carbon Cycle for $50*. His or her partner then takes that card and begins giving clues about each word on the list (without saying any part of that word), trying to get the teammate to say as many of the listed words as possible within one minute.

c. The player giving clues must do so in sequence and may not continue to the next word on the list until his or her teammate says the correct answer or until either player says *pass*. If they pass on a word, they cannot go back later to guess it.

d. The team earns money for each correct answer:
   - $50 category: $10 per correct answer + $50 bonus for all five answers.
   - $100 category: $20 per correct answer + $100 bonus for all five answers.
   - $150 category: $30 per correct answer + $150 bonus for all five answers.

e. Then the other team takes a turn. Teams continue to take turns until all the cards are used. The team with the most money wins the game.

4. After students finish the game, have them use index cards and reference materials to make a new set of game cards. Have them exchange cards with another group and play the game again.

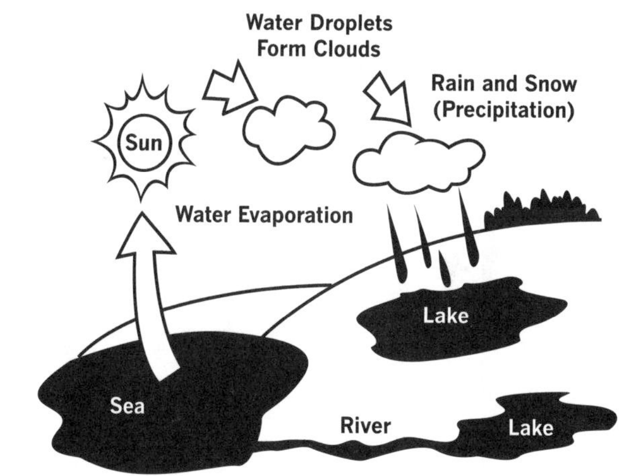

Extended Learning

- Have students draw and label the different Earth cycles in their science notebooks, or have them work together to make posters of the cycles for the classroom.
- Invite students to write and present a fictitious news report about a sudden change in one of the cycles and how that change affects life on Earth.

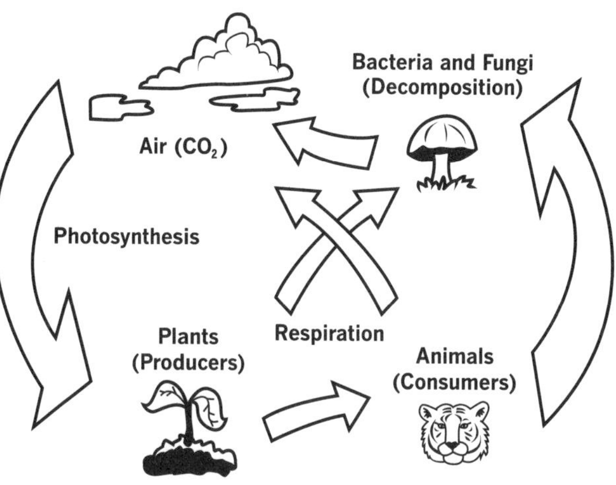

Earth Cycles Pyramid Game Cards

$150 **Nitrogen Cycle**	**1.** decomposer **2.** mineralization **3.** nitrification **4.** nitrogen fixation **5.** denitrification	**$50** **Water Cycle**	**1.** clouds **2.** runoff **3.** evaporation **4.** condensation **5.** precipitation
$100 **Rock Cycle**	**1.** igneous **2.** sedimentary **3.** metamorphic **4.** volcano **5.** magma	**$50** **Carbon Cycle**	**1.** photosynthesis **2.** respiration **3.** producer **4.** consumer **5.** decomposer
$100 **Atmospheric Cycle**	**1.** warm front **2.** low pressure **3.** storm **4.** high pressure **5.** cold front	**$50** **Plate Tectonics**	**1.** subduction **2.** convergent **3.** earthquake **4.** volcano **5.** continental drift

Earth Mind Link

Objective

Students will learn about different time periods and organisms in Earth's history.

Throughout time, climatic conditions have led to dramatic changes on Earth. Those periods, and the organisms that existed during those periods, are grouped into distinct geological eras in Earth's history. In this game, students review facts about these different time periods as they form a "mind link" with their partners.

Materials

- Earth Mind Link reproducible
- index cards
- stopwatches or other timers

1. Invite students to brainstorm historical geological topics as you list their ideas on the board. For example: *Jurassic Period, Cambrian Period, Ice Age, atmospheric conditions, prehistoric man, fossils, mass extinctions, formation of Earth, structure of Earth.* Explain that they will play a game in which partners try to think of the same words for a given topic about Earth's history.
2. Demonstrate by writing the word *dinosaur* on the board and having students secretly write a word pertaining to dinosaurs. Then write your own word about dinosaurs on the board and invite students to share if their word matches yours.
3. Invite students to find a partner and get into groups of six or eight. Give each student a copy of the **Earth Mind Link reproducible (page 83)**, and give each group eight index cards to make eight different topic cards about Earth's history.
4. Then model and explain the rules of the game *Earth Mind Link*:
   a. Partners sit back-to-back, facing outward and keeping their eyes on their own paper.
   b. One player in the group selects a card from the stack and reads it aloud for all players to write on their game sheets for Topic 1.

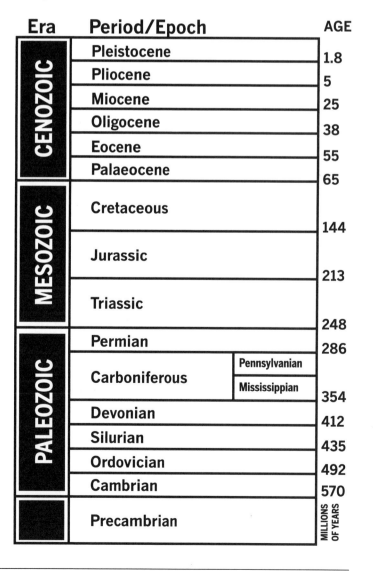

Era	Period/Epoch		AGE (MILLIONS OF YEARS)
CENOZOIC	Pleistocene		1.8
	Pliocene		5
	Miocene		25
	Oligocene		38
	Eocene		55
	Palaeocene		65
MESOZOIC	Cretaceous		144
	Jurassic		213
	Triassic		248
PALEOZOIC	Permian		286
	Carboniferous	Pennsylvanian	
		Mississippian	354
	Devonian		412
	Silurian		435
	Ordovician		492
	Cambrian		570
	Precambrian		

c. Players have one minute to secretly brainstorm words about that topic. They may not communicate with their partner or any other player.
d. After time is up, partners compare answers. They earn one point for every match (in any order).
e. The game continues with the next chosen topic.
f. After eight rounds, the pair of students with the most points wins the game.

5. Invite students to play the game. Check that they understand the rules and monitor them as they play. Make sure partners are not communicating while they brainstorm words.
6. Give students another copy of the reproducible. Invite them play the game again using Earth Mind Link topic cards made by another group.

Extended Learning

- Have students play this game using other science topics or other subjects.
- Have students research and present a pictorial about how fossils are made.
- Arrange a field trip to a nearby archeological dig. Encourage students to write their own list of research questions to "dig up" and answer during the trip.

Topic 1: Ice Age
mastodon
mammoth
saber-toothed tiger
dire wolf
glaciers
2 points

Topic 1: Ice Age
North America
Eurasia
Pleistocene
mammoth
saber-toothed tiger
2 points

Name ______________________________ Date ______________

Earth Mind Link

Directions: Can you read your partner's mind? Choose a topic about Earth's history and write it in the chart. Then brainstorm words about it. Compare your list with your partner's list. How many words match?

Topic 1:	**Topic 2:**	**Topic 3:**	**Topic 4:**
Topic 5:	**Topic 6:**	**Topic 7:**	**Topic 8:**

Solar System Scramble

Materials

- index cards
- scissors
- paper lunch bags
- timers
- lined paper

Objectives

Students will describe equipment needed for space travel.
Students will identify and describe different aspects of our solar system, including the sun, planets, meteorites, comets, asteroids, and other celestial bodies.

In this game, students review facts about the solar system and space travel by thinking of unique vocabulary words that begin with a chosen letter for a given category. They must stretch their minds to think of both unique and correct words.

1. Give each team of four to six students the following supplies: 40 index cards, two paper bags, scissors, a timer, and lined paper to use as record sheets. Have them cut ten of the index cards in half and use them to make 20 alphabet cards for each letter except *Q*, *U*, *V*, *X*, *Y*, and *Z*. Have them place the alphabet cards in one of the bags.
2. On the remaining 30 cards, have students write different categories about the solar system and space travel. For example: *comets, planets, Earth, Mars, sun, moon, satellite, shuttle, astronaut.* Have them put those cards in their other bag.
3. Introduce the game by writing *Planets* and the letter *M* on the board. Ask: *What word about planets can you think of that starts with the letter **M**?* Tell students to secretly write down a word, encouraging them to think of a word that is both correct and unique. Then have students take turns saying their word while the rest of the class raises their hands and checks off the word if they wrote it too. Afterward, ask: *Does anyone have a word that no one else wrote?* Tell students that they are going to play a game in which they earn points for correct, unique words.
4. Model and explain the rules of Solar System Scramble:
    a. Each team chooses five category cards from their bag. All players write those categories on their record sheet. Then the team chooses one letter card.
    b. Players have 15 seconds to write five words, one for each category, that begin with the chosen letter.
    c. When time is up, players take turns reading aloud their words and checking off those they have in common.

978-1-4129-5925-4

d. Any player with a correct word not written by anyone else wins a point.

e. Players then put all the cards back into the bags and repeat the process.

f. After five rounds, the player with the most points wins.

5. Suggest that teams trade category cards and play again, or have them expand the game by adding more categories. You might also reassign students to different groups or play a team tournament of champions!

Extended Learning

- Have students produce and present futuristic travel brochures for different planets in our solar system, including both factual and creative ideas and illustrations.
- Ask students to research a NASA mission and then perform a skit about it. Encourage them to design and create props and backdrops for their skit.
- Have students investigate a specific space career and present a persuasive commercial encouraging people to pursue that career.

Roger Rock

Materials
- sentence strips

Objectives
Students will summarize the rock cycle and compare different rocks.
Students will explain how the rock cycle connects with other Earth systems.

Rocks are classified as *igneous, sedimentary,* or *metamorphic,* depending on how they are formed. Throughout time, they are continuously recycled and transformed in a process known as the *rock cycle,* driven by Earth's tectonic plates. In this game, students follow the comical transformations of Roger Rock.

1. On separate sentence strips, write two identical sets of the following category titles and sentences:

   Igneous Rocks
   - These rocks are formed deep within the earth where temperatures are very high.
   - The intrusive (plutonic) type of these rocks is formed when magma (molten rock inside the earth) cools and crystallizes slowly beneath the earth's surface.
   - The extrusive (volcanic) type of these rocks is formed when magma erupts at the surface as lava and then cools quickly.

   Sedimentary Rocks
   - These rocks are the majority of all rocks on the earth.
   - These rocks are formed from weathering and erosion.
   - These rocks are often layered.
   - These rocks are usually pieces, or sediments, pressed and cemented together.
   - These rocks are often porous between their pieces.
   - These rocks often contain fossils.

   Metamorphic Rocks
   - These rocks are the result of preexisting rock transformation.
   - These rocks form deep within the earth, where extreme temperature, pressure, and chemical reactions cause their transformation.
   - These rocks begin to form at about 12–16 km below the earth's surface.
   - These rocks begin to form at about 100–800 °C.
   - Originating from Canada, the Acasta Gneiss outcrop is the oldest known form of these rocks, dating back almost four billion years.

2. Divide the class into two teams and have each team race to sort a set of sentence strips correctly. Record the time it takes for each

978-1-4129-5925-4

team to complete the race. Add five seconds for each incorrect answer and announce the winners.

3. Explain to students that they will use the facts they have just sorted, along with their imaginations, to complete a creative, collaborative activity called Roger Rock. Divide the class into groups of three and have students in each group choose a different type of rock—igneous, sedimentary, or metamorphic. The goal of each team is to write three factual, yet humorous stories about Roger Rock's adventures in the rock cycle:
   a. Students each begin their own story, describing Roger Rock as their chosen type of rock.
   b. After ten minutes of writing, teammates pass papers and continue each other's stories. They should include facts about Roger Rock that relate to their assigned rock type.
   c. After another ten minutes, teammates pass papers again and finish their stories.
4. Announce the times for students to pass papers. Encourage them to be creative when describing their character's "rocky" adventures. Remind students that their part of the story must tie in with what has already been written.
5. Invite students to read aloud their finished stories. Have the class vote for a winner in each of these categories: funniest story, story that best teaches the rock cycle, most creative story, best plot twist, most creative ending.

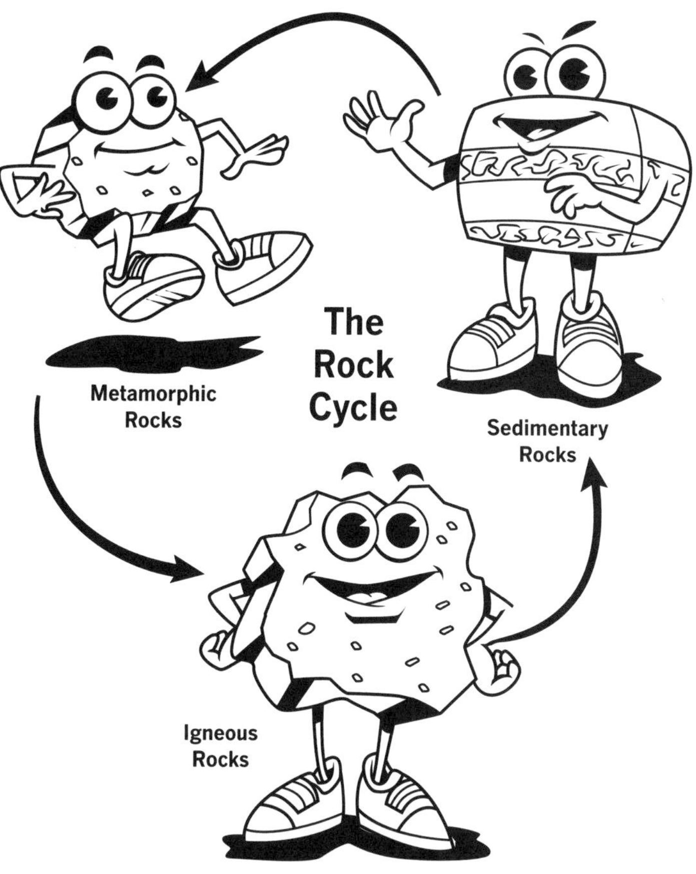

Extended Learning

- Invite a geologist to speak about rock formation and classification.
- Invite students to sing the "Rock Cycle Song" found at: *http://www.chariho.k12.ri.us/curriculum/MISmart/ocean/rocksong.htm.* Challenge them to write and perform their own versions.
- Ask students to make edible models of sedimentary rocks to share with their classmates. Have them tell about their models before they eat the rocky treats.

Epoch Card Game

Materials

- index cards
- references materials about Earth's history

Objectives

Students will research and review important historical geologic events.
Students will match events to the time periods in which they occurred.

In this game, students match time periods in Earth's history with events that happened during those time periods. The game may also be expanded to include a variety of other science topics for a more comprehensive review.

1. As a warm-up for the game, invite students to brainstorm major events that happened during Earth's history. Encourage them to think of monumental events from each period, such as the extinction of dinosaurs, the appearance of new life forms, the formation of new continents, and notable natural disasters.
2. Have each team of three to five students make a set of 40 pairs of matching game cards that include the name of a time period on one card and a corresponding event from that period on another. Invite them to use reference materials to help write the cards. Display the following list (in random order) as examples:

Holocene First modern human beings	**Triassic** First dinosaurs
Miocene First hominids	**Cretaceous** Dinosaurs peak
Precambrian First single-celled organisms	**K-T Boundary** Dinosaur extinction
Cambrian First trilobites	

3. Invite each team to use their cards to play an epoch-matching game. Model and explain the rules:
   a. The dealer deals five cards to each player and places the remaining cards facedown in a stack. He or she turns over the top card to start a discard pile.
   b. Players take turns placing their matching pairs of cards (time period and corresponding event) faceup on the table.
   c. Players must then take a card from either the discard pile or the facedown stack and discard one of their other cards.

d. If the newly selected card matches a card in their hand, players may also put down that pair of matching cards during the same turn.

e. The game continues until one player has matched and put down all of his or her cards on the table to win the game.

4. After students finish the game, have them trade cards with another group and play again. You might also encourage them to play other matching games with their cards. For example, have players place all cards facedown in rows and take turns flipping over pairs of cards to try to find matches.

Extended Learning

- Have students research and report on mass extinctions that have happened during Earth's history, finding out what types of organisms were affected and summarizing what scientists believe were the causes of those extinctions.
- Assign each student group to a particular time period. Ask group members to make a fantasy "time travel" board game or travel brochure about living during that time period. Suggest that they include types of things travelers might see, the climate they might encounter, and possible dangers they could face during their visit.

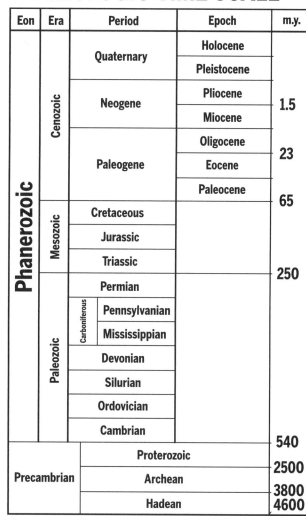

GEOLOGIC TIME SCALE

Eon	Era	Period	Epoch	m.y.
Phanerozoic	Cenozoic	Quaternary	Holocene	
			Pleistocene	
		Neogene	Pliocene	1.5
			Miocene	
		Paleogene	Oligocene	23
			Eocene	
			Paleocene	65
	Mesozoic	Cretaceous		
		Jurassic		
		Triassic		250
	Paleozoic	Permian		
		Carboniferous: Pennsylvanian		
		Carboniferous: Mississippian		
		Devonian		
		Silurian		
		Ordovician		
		Cambrian		540
Precambrian	Proterozoic			2500
	Archean			3800
	Hadean			4600

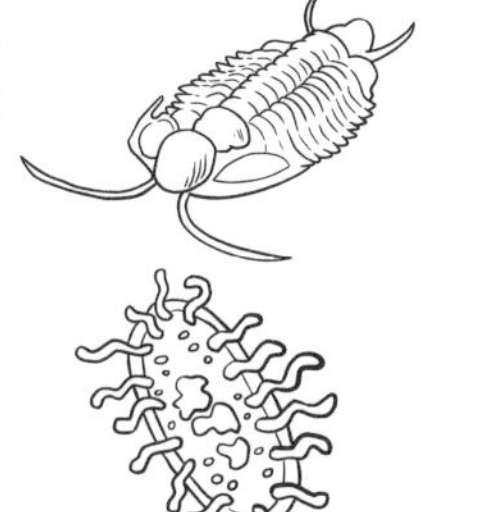

Earth and Space Trivia

Materials

- Earth & Space Trivia Game Board reproducible
- Earth & Space Trivia Game Pieces reproducible
- cardstock
- scissors
- tape
- colored pencils or markers
- index cards
- game pieces
- dice
- reference materials about earth and space science

Objective

Students will write and answer questions about earth and space science, including questions about planets, stars, space travel, Earth's history, weather, and geology.

For this game, students test their knowledge of earth and space science as they answer trivia questions in pursuit of winning colored game pieces. This game may be adapted to include a review of any subject area or a cumulative review of science.

1. Give each group of two to four students a copy of the **Earth & Space Trivia Game Board** and **Earth & Space Trivia Game Pieces reproducibles (pages 92–94)** photocopied onto cardstock. Have them cut out the Player's Stars and color and tape together the two parts of the game board.
2. Tell students that they will play a trivia game in which they must answer questions in six different categories: *Planets, Stars and Constellations, Space Travel, Earth's History, Atmosphere and Weather,* and *Geology.* Write the categories on the board for students to copy onto their Color Key at the top of the game board. They must also decide which color (purple, red, orange, blue, green, yellow) goes with each category.
3. Refer students to the sample trivia card on the Earth & Space Trivia Game Pieces reproducible. Explain that each trivia card should have six different questions, one for each science category indicated by the colored circles. Tell students to color the circles to match the Color Key. The question a player answers is the one that matches the colored space he or she lands on during the game.
4. Have each group use index cards and reference materials to make at least 50 trivia cards. Remind them to refer to their sample trivia card as a guide.
5. Demonstrate how to play the game with a volunteer and explain the rules as follows:
   a. To start the game, all players put their game piece in the center of the game board. They shuffle and place the trivia cards in a facedown stack.
   b. Players take turns rolling one die and moving their game piece the corresponding number of spaces in any direction on the game board.

978-1-4129-5925-4

c. Players must answer a trivia question for the color on which they land. Another player takes a card from the stack, reads aloud the corresponding question, and then checks to see if the answer is correct.

d. If the player answers incorrectly, the next player gets a turn. If the player answers correctly, he or she get to roll again. If the correct answer is also on a star space (corner box), the player gets to color one section of his or her Player's Star. (They should use the same color indicated by the question.)

e. If players land back in the center of the game board, they may pick any category.

f. To win the game, players must correctly answer questions for all colored star spaces to complete their Player's Star. After successfully landing on and answering a question for each category, they should color one section of their Player's Star.

g. The first player to color all six sections of his or her Player's Star wins the game.

6. Monitor students as they play, checking for understanding. Make sure students are following the rules and displaying good sportsmanship.

7. After students play the game, encourage them to exchange cards with another group and play again.

Extended Learning

- Encourage students to create another version of the game by using other categories and game cards.
- Have students design and demonstrate science projects about earth or space science. Some possible projects include: build a working model of a volcano; create a display of local rocks and/or minerals; construct and use unique weather instruments; construct and test a telescope; organize a campaign to help alleviate a local pollution problem; create an earth science Web page.

Name ______________________________ Date ______________

Earth & Space Trivia Game Board

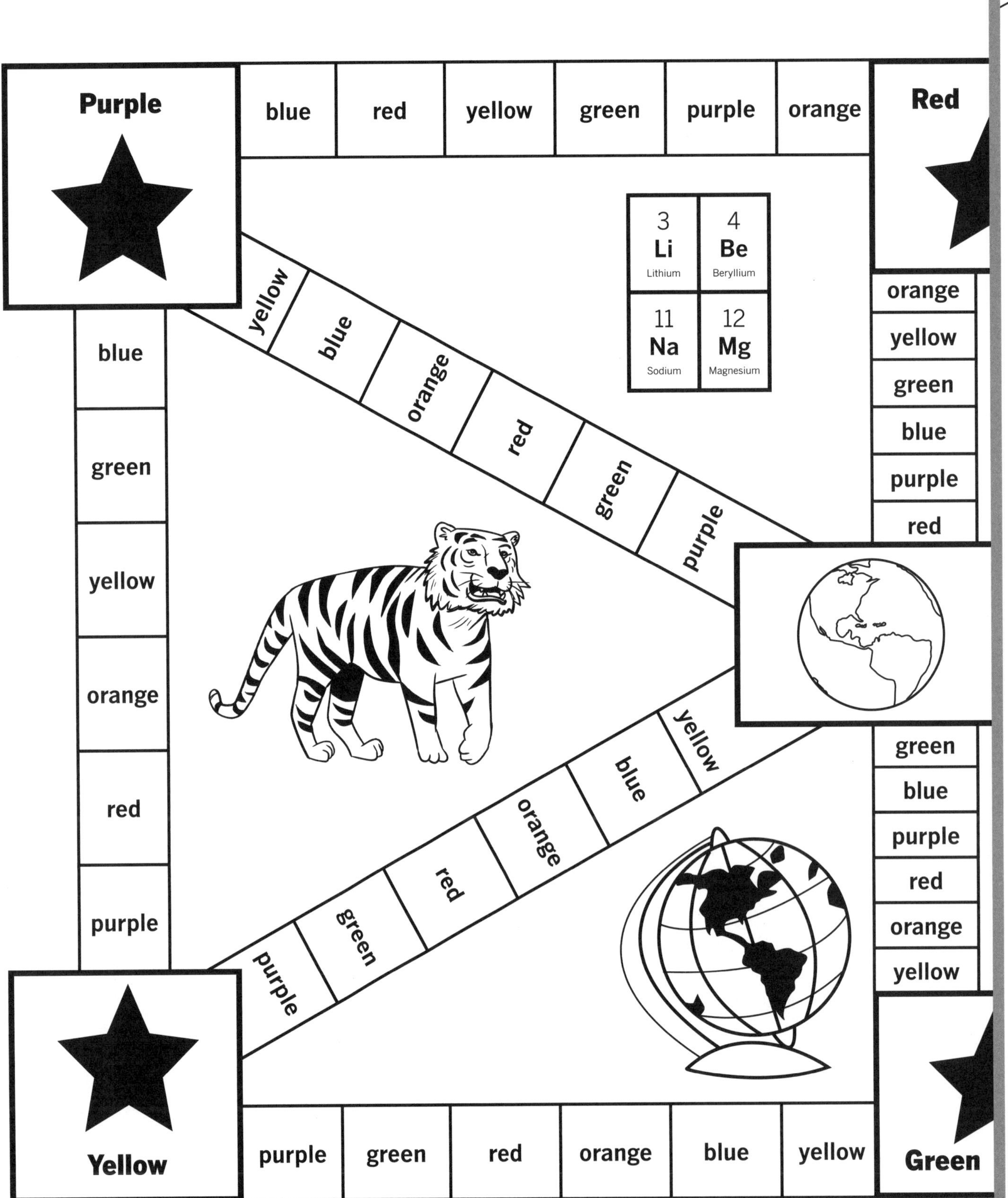

 978-1-4129-5925-4 • © Corwin Press

Color Key *(Fill in the colors and categories.)*

○ ____________________ ○ ____________________

○ ____________________ ○ ____________________

○ ____________________ ○ ____________________

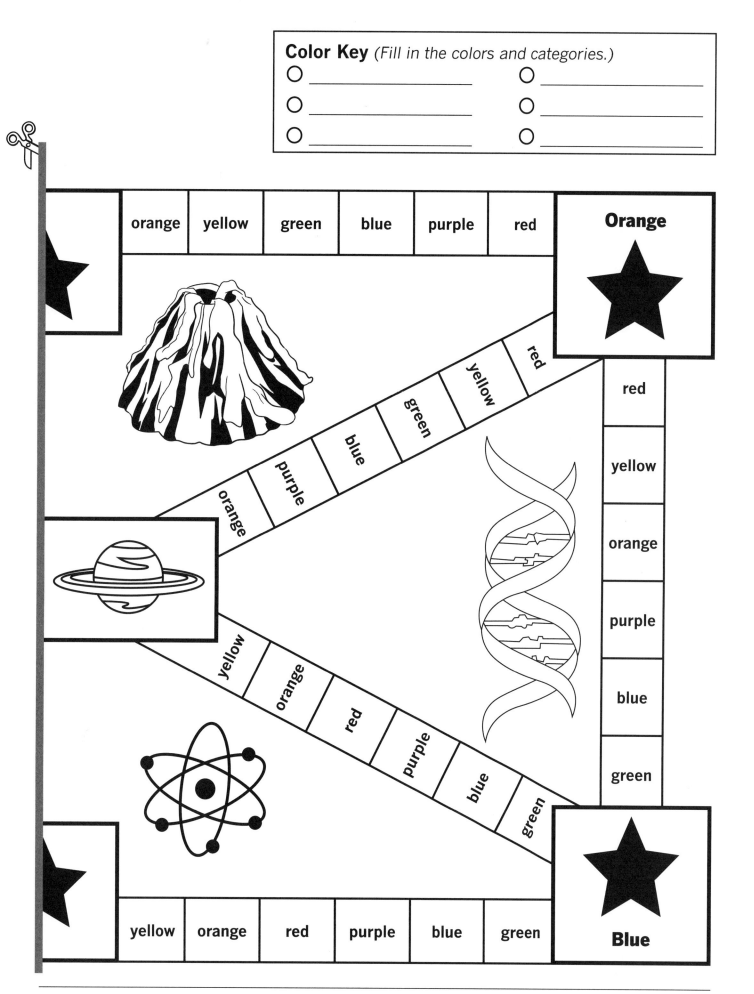

orange | yellow | green | blue | purple | red

Orange

red | yellow | green | blue | purple | orange

red | yellow | orange | purple | blue | green

yellow | orange | red | purple | blue | green

yellow | orange | red | purple | blue | green

Blue

Earth & Space Trivia Game Pieces

Directions: Use this sample game card and Player's Stars to play Earth and Space Trivia.

Sample Game Card

- ○ **Q:** Which element gives Mars its reddish-orange color?
  A: iron
- ○ **Q:** What is another name for a stellar explosion?
  A: supernova
- ○ **Q:** What must a space shuttle overcome in order to propel from Earth?
  A: the force of gravity
- ○ **Q:** What do we call a scientist who studies dinosaur fossils?
  A: paleontologist
- ○ **Q:** What word, when added to the end of a cloud's name, means "rain"?
  A: nimbus
- ○ **Q:** When magma cools and hardens, what kind of rock does it form?
  A: igneous rock

Player's Stars

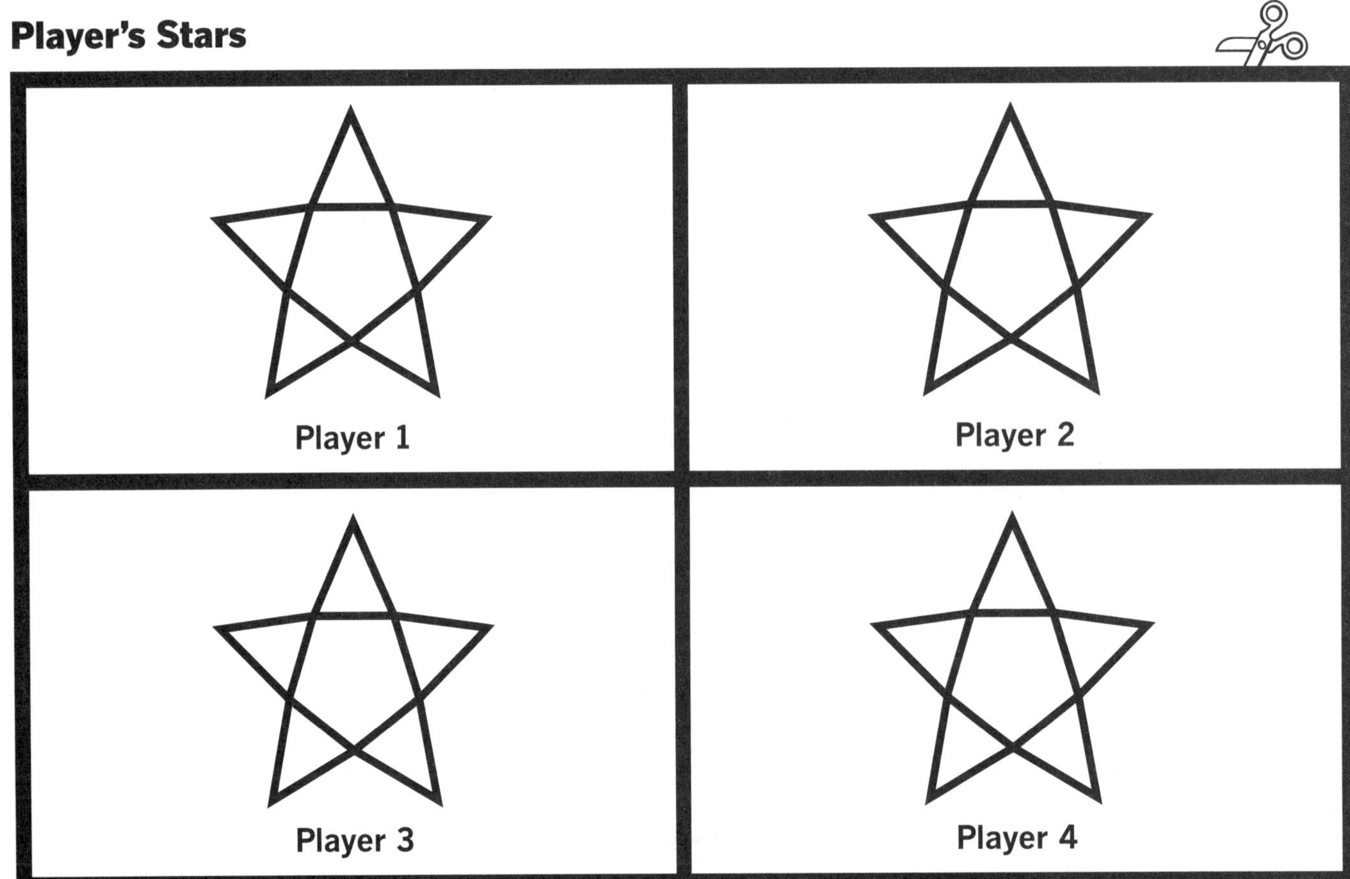

Answer Key

LABORATORY SCAVENGER HUNT (PAGE 10)

1. balance scale
2. fire blanket or safety shower
3. microscope or magnifying glass
4. lab apron or lab coat
5. thermometer
6. beaker, graduated cylinder, or Erlenmeyer flask
7. mortar and pestle
8. fire extinguisher
9. Bunsen burner or hot plate
10. goggles

ORGAN PICTURE CHARADES (PAGE 56)

1. brain
2. liver
3. lung
4. eye
5. muscle
6. skin
7. small intestine
8. bladder

HOMEOSTASIS MILLIONAIRE (PAGE 62)

$100: b. homeostasis
$200: a. regulation
$300: b. 98.6 °F
$500: c. increase body temperature
$1,000: d. negative feedback loop

HUMAN BODY QUIZ SHOW (PAGE 65)

Body Structure

$100: What is the skeleton?
$200: What is the femur?
$300: What are 26 vertebrae?
$400: What are red marrow and yellow marrow?
$500: What are the ball-and-socket joint, pivot joint, hinge joint, and gliding joint?

Organ Systems

$100: What is the bladder?
$200: What are four?
$300: What are the kidneys?
$400: What is the epiglottis?
$500: What are bronchi?

Cells and Genetics

$100: What is a zygote?
$200: What is tissue?
$300: What is "in chromosomes"?
$400: What are alleles?
$500: What are adenine, cytosine, guanine, and thymine?

Diseases and Defenses

$100: What is an infectious disease?
$200: What are white blood cells?
$300: What is diabetes?
$400: What is "produce antibodies"?
$500: What are bacteria, viruses, fungi, and protists?

Health and Nutrition

$100: What are carbohydrates?
$200: What is vitamin A?
$300: What is the category of Fats, Oils, and Sweets?
$400: What are calories?
$500: What are carbohydrates, proteins, fats, vitamins, minerals, and water?

References

BBC Science and Nature. (2004, May 4). *Human body and mind.* Retrieved March 3, 2007, from http://www.bbc.co.uk/science/humanbody/body/index.shtml?organs.

Beyers, J. (1998). The biology of human play. *Child Development*, *69*(3), 599–600.

Cells Alive! (2007, February 17). *Cell models.* Retrieved February 28, 2007, from http://www.cellsalive.com/cells/3dcell.htm.

Collins, A., Guralnick, R., & Speer, B. (2003, January 7). *Take our web geological time machine.* Retrieved March 6, 2007, from the University of California Museum of Paleontology Web site: http://www.ucmp.berkeley.edu/help/timeform.html.

Energy Information Administration. (2006, October). *Energy basics 101.* Retrieved February 27, 2007, from http://www.eia.doe.gov/basics/energybasics101.html.

Gardner, H. (1983). *Frames of mind: The theory of multiple intelligences*. New York, NY: Basic Books.

Jensen, E. (2001). *Arts with the brain in mind*. Alexandria, VA: Association for Supervision and Curriculum Development.

KidsCosmos.org. (2006, September 18). *Kid's cosmos.* Retrieved March 6, 2007, from http://www.kidscosmos.org/kid-stuff.html.

Kious, J., & Tilling, R. (2007, January 30). *This dynamic earth: The story of plate tectonics.* Retrieved March 6, 2007, from the U.S. Geological Survey (USGS) Web site: http://pubs.usgs.gov/gip/dynamic/dynamic.html.

McCarthy, B. (1990). Using the 4MAT system to bring learning styles to schools. *Educational Leadership, 48*(2), 31–37.

National Institute of Health, Office of Science Education. (1999). *Human genetic variation.* Retrieved March 1, 2007, from http://science.education.nih.gov/supplements/nih1/genetic/default.htm.

National Research Council. (1996). *National science education standards*. Washington, DC: National Academy Press.

Natural Resources Canada. (2005, November 22). *Minerals and metals: A world to discover.* Retrieved March 3, 2007, from http://www.nrcan.gc.ca/mms/scho-ecol/treas/oht_e.htm.

NOVA. (2004, July). *Origins: A brief history of life.* Retrieved March 8, 2007, from http://www.pbs.org/wgbh/nova/origins/life.html.

Ranken Energy Corporation. (2006, January 30). *Products made from petroleum.* Retrieved March 5, 2007, from http://www.ranken-energy.com/Products%20from%20Petroleum.htm.

Resource Area for Teachers (RAFT). (2004). *Give it a spin! The world's best, simplest game spinner*. Retrieved February 16, 2007, from http://www.raft.net/ideas/Give%20it%20a%20Spin.pdf.

Science NetLinks. (2000, December 6). *Converting energy*. Retrieved February 27, 2007, from http://www.sciencenetlinks.com/lessons.cfm?BenchmarkID=4&DocID=153.

Tate, M. L. (2003). *Worksheets don't grow dendrites: 20 instructional strategies that engage the brain.* Thousand Oaks, CA: Corwin Press.

ThinkQuest Junior. (2000, March). *This planet really rocks! All about rocks and minerals.* Retrieved March 8, 2007, from http://library.thinkquest.org/J002289/index.html.

University of Washington, Department of Genome Sciences. (2005, April 19). *The genetics project*. Retrieved March 1, 2007, from http://chroma.gs.washington.edu/outreach/genetics/index.html.

Westbroek, G. (2000, June 15). *The history of scientific classification.* Retrieved March 1, 2007, from the Utah State Office of Education Web site: http://www.usoe.k12.ut.us/CURR/Science/sciber00/7th/classify/sciber/history.htm.

Wolfe, P. (2001). *Brain matters: Translating research into classroom practice.* Alexandria, VA: Association for Supervision and Curriculum Development.

Wong, A. (2007, February 25). *Adaptations in camels.* Retrieved March 1, 2007, from the VT Aide Web site: http://www.vtaide.com/png/camel-adaptations4.htm.